COMMON
KNOWLEDGE

COMMON KNOWLEDGE

HOW COMPANIES THRIVE
BY SHARING
WHAT THEY KNOW

NANCY M. DIXON

HARVARD BUSINESS SCHOOL PRESS
BOSTON, MASSACHUSETTS

Library of Congress Cataloging-in-Publication Data

Dixon, Nancy M., 1937-
    Common knowledge : how companies thrive by sharing what they know /
    Nancy M. Dixon.
        p. cm.
    Includes bibliographical references and index.
    ISBN 0-87584-904-0 (alk. paper)
        1. Organizational learning.   2. Business enterprises—
    Communication systems.   3. Intellectual cooperation.
    4. Information networks—Economic aspects.   5. Success in
    business.   I. Title.

    HD58.82 .D585 2000
    658.4'5—dc21   99-048879

FOR MY SONS WHOSE LIVES HAVE SO GREATLY ENRICHED MY OWN:
STEPHEN DIXON JOHNSON
RICHARD SCOTT JOHNSON

CONTENTS

ACKNOWLEDGMENTS

In the course of writing this book many organizations opened their doors to me so I could gain a comprehensive understanding of how they were transferring knowledge. I owe a great deal to the individuals who spent time being interviewed and who paved the way to give me access to others in their organizations. In each of these organizations I talked with dozens of people, but it is particularly important to thank: Dar Wolford and Stan Kwiecien at Ford; Greta Lydecker and Gary Fischer at Chevron; Rick Longbrake and Bob Wacker at Texas Instruments; Nick Milton and Kent Greenes at British Petroleum; Johnathan Ungerleider, Ruddy Ruggles, Ralph Poole, Dale Neef, and Mare Rasmussen at Ernst & Young; Cheryl Lamb and Melissie Rumizen at Buckman Labs; Candice Phelan at Lockheed Martin; Raleigh Amos, Fred Dkystra, Tim Horst, and Doug Omichinski at Bechtel; James T. Stensvaag and Ed Guthrie of the U.S. Army; and Stephen Denning and Seth Kahan at The World Bank.

I have had long-term relationships with colleagues at Conoco and I am grateful for their support and the conversations that helped develop these ideas. They include: Sallie Hightower, David Nelson, Dennis Stephen, Mac Curtis, Dennis Wolf, and Brian Hall, among many others.

There are a host of other colleagues who also inspire and encourage my ongoing efforts: Doris Adams, who I can always count on for a careful and thoughtful response; Marie-eve Marchand, whose ideas push my own; Catherine Fitzgerald, whose breadth of knowledge keeps me humble; and Rick Ross, my colleague and sometimes coauthor, who provides very helpful, practical insight.

COMMON
KNOWLEDGE

CHAPTER 1

INTRODUCTION

A GREAT CARTOON IN THE *NEW YORKER* SOME YEARS BACK showed two venerable men, obviously scientists, sitting back to back at their respective desks. One says to the other, "It's just come to my attention that we've both been working on the same problem for the last twenty-five years." The cartoon is funny because of both the truth and the absurdity of the situation. It is not news to organizations that they need to find ways to keep from continually reinventing the wheel. Although aware of the problem, organizations only recently have begun to construct processes that may change the too familiar predicament depicted in the cartoon.

Perhaps organizations are now addressing the issue of knowledge sharing due to their growing awareness of the importance of knowledge to organizational success or perhaps because technology has made the sharing of knowledge more feasible. Whatever the impetus, organizations have started to do more than talk about sharing knowledge—they have begun to put into place the tools and processes that can actually bring it about. Knowledge databases, best practice seminars, technology fairs, cross-functional teams, "Does anyone know . . . ?" e-mails, and groupware, to name but a few knowledge-sharing processes, have the avowed purpose of getting knowledge that exists in one part of the organization put to use in another part of the organization.

THREE MYTHS

Pervading the idea of knowledge sharing are three myths. Perhaps *myth* is the wrong term—maybe they are just assumptions that seem reasonable at first glance, but when acted on send organizations to a dead end. Many of the organizations I studied started with one or more of these assumptions and then had to make corrections to get back on track. The three myths are (1) build it and they will come, (2) technology can replace face-to-face, and (3) first you have to create a learning culture.

BUILD IT AND THEY WILL COME

Managers who want to make the knowledge in their organizations more available often have a mental image of a large warehouse that contains all of that knowledge. They envision those who are looking for knowledge going to the warehouse and taking out what they need. The idea has a lot of intuitive appeal. Knowledge seems so amorphous that the notion of its being documented and located in a central place offers a comforting sense of control and manageability.

The first thing most organizations do is build a central electronic database, a perfect fit for the warehouse image. But, to their dismay, having spent a considerable amount of money to create the database, very little happens: neither contributions nor retrievals occur with much enthusiasm. Bechtel, one of the companies profiled in this book, experienced this with its initial Clearinghouse. The workers at its construction sites sent in very few items and seemed to have little interest in the system. Chevron's Corporate-Wide Data Base for Best Practices also elicited a modest response. Such experiences are a disappointing outcome to a very well intentioned idea.

When organizations find that their members show little interest in the database, they often backtrack in an attempt to "fix" the lack of contributions. The thinking is that an incentive system is needed to reward people for contributing and retrieving knowledge. Incentives have become a fairly familiar second step in knowledge management scenarios. The types of rewards offered have varied from the mundane to the ridiculous—a Dove bar for each time you go into the database, 500 frequent flyer points for every submission. The consulting firm KPMG invented a "give to get" scheme; employees can't take any knowledge out of the system unless they put something in. In some companies the database manager ends up doing a lot of encouraging to get submissions. The manager of Chevron's system, for example, urges people to "send that in," although she still ends up writing many of the submissions herself. The same is true at Bechtel. People in central functions who visit construction sites are more likely to write up an idea themselves, even though they actively encourage engineers at the sites to "send that in, even if it's just written on the back of a napkin." Ernst & Young, like several other consulting firms, has tried to address the issue by putting an item in its performance review form related to contributing to E&Y's Knowledge Web.

Although incentives work to some extent, none of them delivers the hoped-for results. The answer lies not in better incentives but in altering that powerful originating image of the warehouse. That image places the focus on *collecting and storing* knowledge instead of on *reusing* it, which is the ultimate goal. This starting image needs to be transformed into one that focuses on reuse.

TECHNOLOGY CAN REPLACE FACE-TO-FACE

If a group of people who do the same kind of work are brought together, they will begin to share knowledge (although we often think of this as telling "war stories"). That has always been one of the great side benefits of training programs or of attending conferences. But getting people together is costly, because it involves travel and time away from the job—expenses that in this time of cost cutting seem extravagant.

One of the great promises that technology holds is that it can allow people to share knowledge without having to be in the same place. Although this sounds reasonable, it unfortunately just doesn't always work out that way.

All of the knowledge management systems I studied that were initially designed as technology systems have evolved toward being a combination of technology and face-to-face meetings. Ford's Best Practice Replication process is one of the most effective uses of this technology/face-to-face hybrid to share knowledge that I've seen. Best Practice Replication was championed by Dale McKeehan, vice president of Vehicle Operations, in March 1995. McKeehan saw a need for Europe and North America (both in his area of responsibility) to get better at sharing ideas. A team of production engineers was sent from a Vehicle Operations plant in Kansas City to a similar plant in Saarlouis, Germany. The production engineers were there to "walk the line" with their German counterparts to see what was happening in the Saarlouis plant and gather ideas that they could use in the Kansas City plant. Then, a few weeks later, the German team paid a visit to the Kansas City plant to see what *they* could use. Out of these meetings fifteen short-term and thirty long-term best practices were identified. These initial practices became the basis of the Best Practice Replication Database, which has grown to over 600 ideas and now involves all thirty-seven Vehicle Operations plants around the world. In addition to identifying forty-five best practices, something else happened during these initial visits that was perhaps more important. The engineers from the two plants got to know each other; they came to respect each other and to recognize that the other had some very useful ideas that they had not thought of themselves. Stan Kwiecien, Coordinator for Best Practice Replication, Vehicle Operations, says that the system would not have worked without first building trust through face-to-face exchanges and would not continue to work without the quarterly face-to-face exchanges among the production engineers. As evidence of their importance, the quarterly meetings usually produce an immediate jump in submissions to the database.

E&Y is another case in point. The firm has a very sophisticated Knowledge Web that holds some 350,000 items and has up to 3,000 hits a day. But a vast system of face-to-face interaction encourages and supports this technology system. Twenty-two networks of consultants work in particular industries or on particular solutions (e.g., managed care, manufacturing, supply chain operations, new product development). The networks hold frequent face-to-face meetings to learn from each other and to build the relationships that support the Knowledge Web. And as at Ford, a surge in submissions as well as hits on the system always follows a network meeting. Recently, E&Y has moved even farther into the face-to-face realm by "hard-tagging" certain expert consultants in each network to travel around as full-time collectors and disseminators of the knowledge for that network.

Technology has to be married with face-to-face interaction to create the most effective systems; one does not replace the other, although clearly one can greatly enhance the other.

First You Have to Create a Learning Culture

"Our organization has a very competitive culture, so no one is going to tell anyone else something that might help the other person get ahead." The third myth, based on beliefs such as this, is that the exchange of knowledge happens only in organizations that have a noncompetitive or a collaborative culture. It follows that the first thing you have to do is to fix the culture and then get people to share. But I have found that it's the other way around. If people begin sharing ideas about issues they see as really important, the sharing itself creates a learning culture. I have, of course, inserted an important caveat in that sentence: "about issues they see as really important."

Ford supplies an illustration of this point. Every Ford plant is responsible for making a 5 percent productivity increase every year. People in the plants refer to it as the "task." This is serious business; as one plant manager said, "If you don't make your task, your successor will." Year after year it is a real chore to keep making the 5 percent task, and production engineers are stretched to find some new process or technique to reduce the cost of labor, materials, or energy. Now, the Best Practice Replication process sends the production engineer in each Vehicle Operations plant five to eight best practices items a week, each of which describes how a sister plant reduced costs. Each item spells out exactly how much was saved, specified in hours, materials, or energy. The production engineers have come to rely on this system as a way to make their task. In fact, on average, 40 percent of task comes from best practices pulled off the system—and in some plants 100 percent of task is taken from the system. It is significant that this system is so well used in an industry that is known for being highly competitive. People use it because the system offers help with a very critical business need. But what has also happened at Ford as a result of this ongoing exchange is a change in the company's culture. A learning culture is developing based on this experiential understanding of why knowledge sharing is important.

It is a kind of chicken-or-egg issue: Which comes first, the learning culture or the exchange of knowledge? Given many organizations' rather abysmal success rate at changing their culture, I would put my money on having the exchange impact the culture rather than waiting for the culture to change.

SHARING WHAT YOU KNOW

I often hear that it is difficult to get people to share their knowledge, but my experience is quite the opposite: people are very willing to share what they know. I live in Washington D.C., a city that is full of tourists. As it happens, D.C. is a very difficult city to find your way around in, even with a map. And because I normally walk to work I am frequently stopped by tourists who ask, "Isn't the Metro around here somewhere?" "Am I on the right street to reach the Kennedy Center?" "Where is M Street from here?" Not only am I not annoyed at these inquiries,

I am pleased to be asked. I take pleasure in seeing relief light up their faces when I provide directions.

I know that I am not alone in my willingness to share information. People, often complete strangers, offer gratuitous information—conversations in the grocery store like, "I wouldn't get in that line if I were you, it's really moving slow," or someone who comes up to me after I've made a speech to say, "There is an article in yesterday's *Wall Street Journal* about that topic that you might want to check out." The truth is that if we know something that we think someone else needs to know, it is difficult for us to refrain from telling them. It is almost a natural impulse to tell others what we know. Eric Erickson, the great developmental psychologist, said that we are, by nature, "a teaching species."

No less at work. I frequently call colleagues with requests such as "I know you won a grant from the Ford Foundation last year; what can you tell me about that process?" or "What organization do you know that is doing the best job at self-managed teams?" I can't think of a time when I've been told, "Sorry, I can't share that information with you." Colleagues, and even new acquaintances, willingly fax articles, provide names of others to talk with, and take time from busy schedules to tell me what they know. Likewise I receive many such requests, to which I respond as best I can even if they come at an inconvenient time.

So if people are naturally willing to share what they know, what is the origin of the familiar refrain heard in organizations, "It's really hard to get people to share what they know"? I think this comment doesn't refer to the times when you phone a colleague or send out a "does anyone know . . ." e-mail. Most people's reactions are like mine: they are flattered to be asked and respond as fully as they can. When we hear this complaint it nearly always refers to getting people to "write up something" to send into a database—and that is a very different thing.

When David Constant, Sara Kiesler, and Lee Sproull did a study of attitudes about information sharing, they found that people distinguished between what they had learned through their own experience, such as how to fix a software bug, and more tangible information, such as documents.[1] They viewed the less tangible things almost as part of their identity and self-worth. They were willing to share the tangible documents and programs because they belonged to the organization. Although they were equally willing to share both, their motivation for sharing the less tangible information was markedly different. They shared this type of information because they gained some personal benefit from doing so. That personal benefit might have been no more than having others acknowledge their expertise, or the smile they got in return—but they got something back.

The findings of that study go a long way toward explaining why we willingly respond to a request for information from a colleague who leans over the cubicle wall and why we may be less enthusiastic about writing that same knowledge up for a database. Little personal benefit comes from contributing to a database that is accessed by others with whom I have no connection and moreover from whom I am unlikely to hear. A database is like a black hole. It gives nothing back—no thank you, no smile, no sigh of relief, no enthusiasm on the other end of the line.

The term "share," which we use so frequently when we talk about an exchange of knowledge, may seem a strange choice of words, and somewhat out of place among such mechanistic terms of knowledge management as "capture," "disseminate," and "transfer." "Share" feels like an anomaly, a throwback to the sixties, when we were all "sharing our thinking." But the term quite rightly recognizes the personal nature of the knowledge that is gained from work experience. What I have learned from my work experience, from the wildly successful projects of which I am inordinately proud, as well as from the very painful failures, is very much a part of who I am. To recall the actions I took is to recall as well the strong sense of pride I experienced or the nagging anxiety that is associated with each. What I "know" from these experiences, I know at a very deep level. I can, of course, tease out of that mixture of fact and feeling a rational set of "how-to steps" or a definitive list of "cautions," but the "knowing" is deeply personal and to ask me to share it is to ask me to give something of myself.

One of the best examples of making use of our natural willingness to share is British Petroleum's Peer Assist Program.

Peer Assist enables a team that is working on a project to call upon another team (or a group of individuals) that has had experience in the same type of task. The teams meet face-to-face for one to three days in order to work through an issue the first team is facing. For example, a team that is drilling in deep water off the coast of Norway can ask for an "assist" from a team that has had experience in deep-water drilling in the Gulf of Mexico. As the label implies, "assists" are held between peers, not with supervisors or corporate "helpers." The idea of Peer Assists was put forward by a corporate task force in late 1994, and BP wisely chose to offer it as a simple idea without specifying rules or lengthy "how-to" steps. It is left up to the team asking for the assistance to specify who it would like to work with, what it wants help on, and at what stage in the project it could use the help.

If we want people in our organizations to share what they have learned, we would be wise to create the conditions in which sharing results is of personal benefit. Certainly, personal benefit is to be gained from doing a Peer Assist. Those who offer their knowledge feel honored to be asked. Being selected to assist is an acknowledgment of their expertise. Those who receive the assistance also share what they know. They feel respected for the knowledge they have drawn together and for their analysis and interpretation. They recognize that the people who have come to assist leave even more knowledgeable than when they came because of the exchange.

Like many English words, *share* has two meanings; it means to give away a part, which is an act of generosity, and it means to hold in common, as in a "shared belief system." These seemingly different meanings merge in the context of knowledge management. If I share my knowledge, that is, give it away, then we can both hold it in common—common knowledge that is known throughout the organization.

WHAT'S IN A NAME?

What a knowledge-sharing system is called really makes a difference. Bechtel started out asking employees at all construction sites to send in the lessons they had learned. But after a few months of sparse response the company realized that "lessons learned" meant "mistakes" to these construction employees. They felt they were being asked to reveal what had gone wrong and were reluctant to make themselves look bad. The British version, "lessons learnt," used at British Petroleum seems to carry the same troublesome implications. On the other hand, the term "best practice" also has many problems, and Ford regrets that it opted to use it. Some production engineers are reluctant to send in a practice because they're not sure it is really "best," while others say to themselves, "Well, if they already have a *best* for that process, I guess there's no need to send this one in." Chevron, which has had a similar difficulty with the term, now includes a caveat in all its information: "Don't let *best* get in the way of *better*," to try to keep employees from getting hung up on whether something is really "best." But for most people, the terms themselves have such strong connotations that caveats have little impact. Some companies have gone to using "leading practice" as a way around the "best" difficulty. E&Y asks consulting teams to send in "naturally occurring work products," which means those documents that are produced in the course of a consulting engagement. But that term, which is an accurate reflection of what E&Y collects, is too limited for others to use.

The difficulty, of course, is that any term an organization chooses carries some baggage. Even the term "knowledge management" has unwanted implications. The "management" part implies that this is something Management is in charge of, when what is wanted is that everyone in the organization be involved in the exchange as well as the generation of knowledge. "Knowledge management" inspires thoughts of "another management fad."

Some of the most serviceable names don't mention knowledge at all. British Petroleum's Peer Assist places the emphasis on people assisting each other but leaves out the specifications as to what assistance is given. Likewise, BP's Virtual Team Network puts the emphasis on working together as a team.

A useful resolution to the naming dilemma is to find a term

that signifies what is to be accomplished rather than delineating the type or quality of knowledge to be shared. It is better yet if the emphasis is placed on the outcome rather than the process, and on the user rather than the information itself. Where "lessons learned database" conveys the idea "input what you have learned," Peer Assist says "if you need assistance try this." That may be a subtle difference, but as we have seen these subtle differences impact how people react to such systems. RW Johnson Pharmaceutical Research echoes that idea in urging "Don't call it knowledge management. Link it to the Business!"

Defining Common Knowledge

This book focuses on only one of the many possible types of knowledge that reside in an organization: the knowledge that employees learn from doing the organization's tasks. I call this kind of knowledge "common knowledge" to differentiate it from book knowledge or from lists of regulations or databases of customer information. Some examples of common knowledge are what an organization has learned about how to introduce a new drug into the diabetes market, how to increase refinery reliability, how to reduce materials cost on capital projects, and how to control the amount of pitch in wood pulp.

These examples all start with "how to" because common knowledge is the "know how" rather than the "know what" of school learning. Moreover, it is "know how" that is unique to a specific company. This very specificity is what gives the knowledge gained from experience its potential to provide an organization with a competitive edge. Although many other kinds of knowledge—for example, customer information and competitor intelligence—must be made broadly available, they have less potential to provide a competitive advantage because the same knowledge is equally available to competitors. The common knowledge that is generated internally, by talented employees in the act of accomplishing the organization's task in new and innovative ways, is where knowledge sharing can really pay off.

Another sense in which the knowledge gained from doing the organization's work is "common" is that across an organization many people have related or very similar "know how." For example, Chevron may have a capital project in Rochester that has done an outstanding job of reducing materials cost and another one in Miami that has also substantially reduced materials cost. Although each may have accomplished the task in a different way, both possess part of Chevron's common knowledge about how to reduce the cost of materials. To exploit this common knowledge, Chevron has created a group it calls Project Resources and given it the task of ensuring that the Rochester project knows what the Miami project team has learned, and vice versa. Through Project Resources, Chevron has made reducing materials costs on capital projects not only common knowledge but held "in common" as well.

A fascinating example of common knowledge comes from the flute making industry.[2] As it happens, three flute companies in the Boston area produce what are regarded by flutists as the best flutes in the world. All three companies—Haynes, Powell, and Brannen—have a common historical antecedent in the Haynes Company, founded in 1900. The flutes are handcrafted by a series of workers who successively drill the tone holes in the tube, solder the key mechanisms, attach the pads, construct the head joint and embouchure hole, and polish, pack, and ship the completed flutes. Each craftsman is skilled in only certain steps of the process, and successive steps are often renegotiated between craftsmen when a developing flute does not have the right "feel." No two flutes are alike, yet flutists can easily differentiate a Powell flute from a Haynes flute by the way it plays. Each company produces flutes with a distinct quality or family resemblance. When craftsmen switch companies (e.g., from Haynes to Brannen), they find they must retrain to learn the new feel. It is the particular common knowledge, learned from years of working at the Haynes company, that makes the Haynes flute unique; the same is true for Powell and Brannen. Each company's unique common knowledge is a critical factor in its success.

For many people, a distinction between knowledge and information is crucial. Information has been defined as data that is "in formation"—that is, data that has been sorted, analyzed, and displayed, and is communicated through spoken language, graphic displays, or numeric tables. Knowledge, by contrast, is defined as the meaningful links people make in their minds between information and its application in action in a specific setting. Linking knowledge to action is a useful way to differentiate it from information, but the distinction gets blurred when applied to organizational situations. For example, a truck manufacturing team in St. Louis has "knowledge" about how to attach the front bumper to a truck in fifteen seconds. When it writes that knowledge up and sends it to a sister factory in Dearborn, it becomes "information" because the team in Dearborn may or may not make the connections to its specific setting. In such a scenario it is difficult to point to something and say, "Oh, that is just information" or "That is knowledge," because how it is classified depends on who is doing the saying. I find myself using the terms somewhat interchangeably, as I have already done in this chapter. For me the critical distinction is between what I am calling "common knowledge," that is, knowledge generated from the experience of people engaged in organizational tasks, and knowledge (or information) that is more theoretical—"know how" as opposed to "know what." Common knowledge is always linked to action. It is derived from action and it carries the potential for others to use it to take action. Whether or not others do take action on the common knowledge depends on the many factors I write about in this book.

What the Book Is About

This book is based on an in-depth look at a number of organizations that are leading the field in knowledge transfer. I wanted to see what these exemplary organizations were doing to make knowledge sharing a reality, and learn how their systems evolved. I was also curious to see if there were underlying principles that could be drawn from all the companies, principles that other organizations could use in developing their own knowledge-sharing systems. In a very real sense I was attempting to gather lessons learned about how organizations are doing lessons learned!

The first year of this two-year study of knowledge sharing was done in cooperation with Ernst & Young's Center for Business Innovation and drew heavily on five organizations: Ford, Chevron, Bechtel, British Petroleum (BP), and E&Y itself. Each organization let me take an in-depth look at what it was doing, allowing me to interview the people who had designed the systems, those who were managing or supporting the systems, those who were marketing the systems internally and externally, and organizational members who were using the processes to get their work done. In addition to the interviews, I was given access to written materials, including submission forms, reports on usage, PowerPoint presentations, and speeches. In several organizations, I was able to explore databases on-line and to sit in on process meetings where knowledge sharing was taking place.

These organizations were pioneers in knowledge sharing, inventing ways to accomplish what others had only been talking about. And because they had few models to rely on, each invented a very different system. All had made mistakes along the way, but I found much to be learned from both their successes and failures. The systems have been in place at the most for three to four years and are continually evolving. That fact came home to me when after four months of data collection at Ford, I wrote up my findings and sent them to Dar Wolford (Manager, Best Practice Replication) for verification, only to be told that two of the processes I was writing about had been merged, a database had been renamed, and a new division within Ford had become involved, all since our last conversation. Clearly the inventing is not over.

After completing the interviews, reviewing the materials provided by the organizations, and conducting a preliminary analysis, I presented my first-year findings at a working conference sponsored by Ernst & Young's Center for Business Innovation. The findings were presented for verification to representatives from the organizations participating in the study. My interpretation was deepened and expanded through the insights they shared with me and this led me to a second year of study that involved a new group of organizations including Texas Instruments, Lockheed Martin, Buckman Labs, and the U.S. Army. From these organizations, and many others, I have learned unique ways of collecting knowledge, odd schemes for rewarding participation, and a few strokes of genius about reuse. I have also had the opportunity to work with a number of organizations that are at the beginning stages of developing processes to share and reuse knowledge. All of these organizations have added to the research base from which I formed the ideas in this book, in addition to concepts relating to both knowledge and learning that I drew from the existing literature.

My major goal in writing this book is to broaden readers' thinking about how a company might share knowledge. Therefore I discuss many ways in which real companies have been successfully transferring knowledge. I will have reached my goal if, by the end of the book, the reader is thinking, "There is a wide variety of ways my company could transfer its most critical knowledge—some that require technology and many that don't." I also hope I have given readers enough details about these transfer processes so that they understand not only *how* these different systems work, but *why* they work.

Another goal is to help readers figure out which of these many systems would be most effective in their own settings—how to tell whether BP's Peer Assist would be more effective than Ford's Best Practice Replication. Most organizations that have implemented some form of knowledge management have had to resort to trial and error to find a transfer system that works for them, which means they have often made costly false starts and gone down time-consuming blind alleys before hitting on what works for the type of knowledge they are trying to transfer. This book offers a more systematic way to make those decisions. By looking at who the intended receiver is, what kind of task is involved, and the type of knowledge to be transferred, it is possible for organizations to construct a transfer system tailored to their particular situations.

CHAPTER 2

CREATING AND LEVERAGING COMMON KNOWLEDGE

IN THE LAST CHAPTER, I USED THE FLUTE-MAKING INDUSTRY AS an example of the competitive advantage that can come from an organization's common knowledge. Fortunately for Haynes, Powell, and Brannen, the flute-making industry changes little over time. That is not so for the rest of us. Most of us work in industries where today's common knowledge will not solve the problems of tomorrow. Organizations must continually reinvent and update their common knowledge. This requires them to engage repeatedly in two kinds of knowledge activities. First, they have to find effective ways to translate their ongoing experience into knowledge—*create* common knowledge. Second, they have to transfer that knowledge across time and space—*leverage* common knowledge.

In this chapter I discuss these two knowledge activities and the criteria that impact whether or not the transfer process will be successful. I end with an overview of the five types of knowledge transfer that will be discussed in more detail in the chapters that follow.

CREATING COMMON KNOWLEDGE

Translating experience into knowledge may seem like something that happens automatically in an organization, but unfortunately it does not. Remember the old joke about the teacher who rather than having twenty years of teaching experience had the same experience twenty times? We all probably know a few people like that. In fact, it takes a certain amount of *intention* to create knowledge out of an experience. This involves a willingness to reflect back on actions and their outcomes before moving forward. In an organization with a bias for action, the time for reflection may be hard to come by. And when it is a team rather than an individual that has produced the outcome, the task of translating experience into knowledge is compounded, because all the team members have to come to some understanding of what happened and why. Many organizations allot no time to debriefing a project team or reviewing a just completed event. A team may have achieved extraordinary success—for example, the introduction of a new product that far exceeded expectations—but the organization finds itself unable to repeat that success because the team has not taken the time to build the knowledge about why it worked so well. The team had the experience but didn't extract knowledge from it.

Figure 2–1 diagrams the steps that a team must take to translate experience into common knowledge. The first step is that a team engages in some task that occurs over a period of weeks or months. Second, the team's work produces an outcome, perhaps successful, perhaps disappointing. A result alone, however, is not enough to create common knowledge. The third step is that the team members take the time to build connections between what they did (their actions) and what the outcome was. This discussion is what translates their experience into knowledge. And if they are a work team that will do the same task again in a few days or months, they will also need a fourth

FIGURE 2-1

FIGURE 2-1

CREATING COMMON KNOWLEDGE

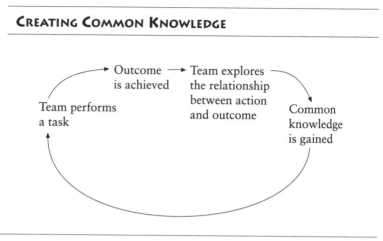

step: to modify their actions the next time, based on the knowledge they have developed. In chapter 3, I will discuss this process in detail and offer examples of organizations that have made translating experience into knowledge a disciplined and effective activity. For now, I want only to emphasize that constructing team knowledge does not happen automatically. It requires a disciplined strategy that is carried out by active participants who are intent not only on getting effective results but also on knowing how they got those results. Without such a strategy, teams make the same mistakes again and again or, what may be worse, are not able to repeat a one-off success.

LEVERAGING COMMON KNOWLEDGE

The second necessary activity is transferring knowledge across time and space. Organizations approach the transfer of knowledge with some justifiable apprehension. The concern is that if time and energy are spent moving existing knowledge from place to place within an organization, there may be less time and energy available for developing new knowledge and the organization may fall behind competitors who are perhaps generating

FIGURE 2-2

LEVERAGING COMMON KNOWLEDGE

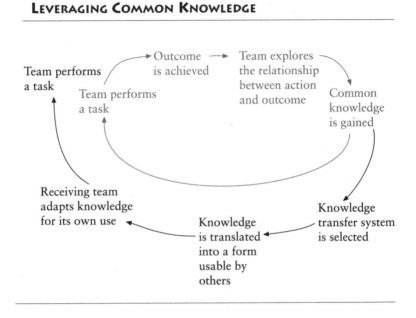

new ideas. On the other hand, exploiting existing knowledge produces enormous cost savings; companies have saved millions by transferring knowledge from one part of the organization to another. Ford claims $34 million were saved in just one year by transferring ideas between Vehicle Operations plants; Texas Instruments saved enough from transferring knowledge between wafer fabrication plants to pay for building a whole new facility; Chevron reduced its costs on capital projects alone by $816 million. In fact, neither transferring common knowledge nor creating new knowledge can be neglected; the first is critical for current viability, the second for future viability.[1] The task is to find an appropriate balance between the two, not to swing fully in one direction or the other.

The transfer of common knowledge begins, of course, with the creation of common knowledge; otherwise there would be nothing to transfer. Thus figure 2–2 builds on figure 2–1 and then adds these steps:

- Find a method for transferring the knowledge to a group or individual that can reuse it.

- Translate what has been learned into a form that others can use.

- The receiving team or individual adapts the knowledge for use in a particular context.

- The process repeats itself with the receiving team taking action on a new task.

The receiving team's action, having been adapted rather than simply adopted, may itself constitute an innovation or at least a stepwise improvement on what the source team was able to do.

How to accomplish the very complex set of steps, illustrated in figure 2–2, of translating experience into knowledge and leveraging it across an organization is the subject of the rest of this book. Most of the examples I use involve *team knowledge* rather than *individual knowledge* because that is where most organizations have focused their knowledge-sharing efforts. As learning theorists John Seely Brown and Paul Duguid have written, "Experience at work creates its own knowledge and as most work is a collective, cooperative venture, so most depositional knowledge is intriguingly collective—less held by individuals than shared by work groups."[2]

ONE SIZE DOESN'T FIT ALL

In the many organizations I have investigated I have found a surprising variety of processes aimed at knowledge transfer. And what was even more unexpected, I discovered that the method that any one organization used to leverage knowledge bore little resemblance to the method any other organization was using, although each organization seemed to swear by its own process. Spending a couple of weeks in one organization, I would begin to identify some principles that made knowledge transfer work. Then I would go on to another organization only to find that none of my carefully thought through principles was present in the new situation. It was quickly evident to me that "one size" does not fit all. I did not find reliable principles of transfer that could be generalized across all organizations and all knowledge management practices.

But in this diversity I began to discern what it was that made a method work in one place but not in another. That more in-depth look led me to focus on the transfer process itself, and I found three criteria that determine how a transfer method will work in a specific situation:

1. Who the intended receiver of the knowledge is in terms of similarity of task and context

2. The nature of the task in terms of how routine and frequent it is

3. The type of knowledge that is being transferred

Figure 2–3 shows these three factors impacting which transfer mechanism is chosen and how knowledge is translated into a usable form. I give an overview of these important three factors here and leave it to later chapters to describe them in greater detail.

WHO THE INTENDED RECEIVER IS

In some organizations the group that is the source of the knowledge and the group that is the intended receiver of the knowledge are doing very similar tasks in very similar contexts. That was certainly true in the Ford plants: no matter what part of the world it existed in, every Ford plant had people responsible for installing brakes and putting in windshields. Some of the plants were able to put the brakes in faster and maybe even better than others. But the tasks were so familiar that an engineer from Dearborn would not need to ask what the team that was installing a windshield in Cincinnati was doing or why. Task similarity between Texas Instruments' wafer fabrication plants was also evident: every plant put layers of electrical interconnects on the wafer, cleaned off the last layer of photochemicals, and

FIGURE 2-3

CRITERIA THAT IMPACT THE TRANSFER PROCESS

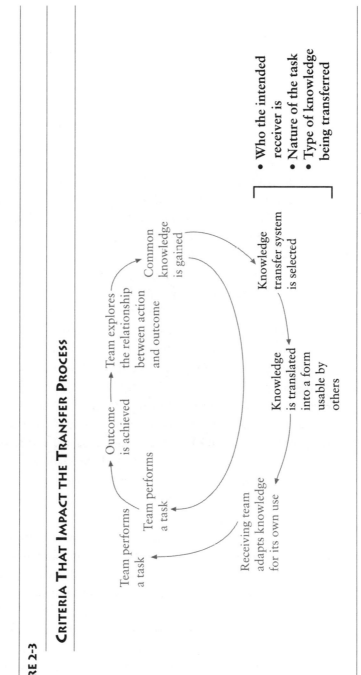

made the wafer ready for the next layer. If a team in Dallas improved its process in a way that provided greater quality, a team in San Jose could easily understand what it had done and why.

But in other organizations tasks and contexts differed greatly from team to team. At Ernst & Young, for example, a consulting team in Boston that was developing a proposal to present to a national association could be engaged in very different activities from a team in Atlanta that was preparing a proposal for a high-tech startup firm. A team member in Atlanta might well ask his colleague in Boston, "Now, why are you doing that?" The overall task might be the same—developing a proposal—but what each team was actually doing might not be recognizable by the other as necessary or well done.

One of the ways that differing contexts can impact the transfer of knowledge has to do with the receiving team's "absorptive capacity."[3] The idea here is that, to learn something new, a team or an individual has to already have enough related knowledge to absorb the new knowledge. It is a little like saying no matter how talented the instructor, students can't learn how to do division if they haven't mastered multiplication. Prior related knowledge in an organizational setting may include basic skills (e.g., the ability to work together as a team or experience with project management), shared language (e.g., medical terms or quality terms), and technical knowledge (e.g., how to install a gas tank or how to develop software). For example, the internal knowledge management consultants at British Petroleum, who are responsible for working with various business units to implement knowledge management, found that they were much more successful when the people in the business unit already had some experience in working together in teams. Knowing how to function as members of a team increased the unit's absorptive capacity to implement knowledge transfer. Research evidence, as well, shows that lack of absorptive capacity in the receiving team is a significant barrier to knowledge transfer.[4]

The similarity of task and context between the source group and the receiving group and the absorptive capacity of the receiving group are deciding factors in determining what kind of transfer method will be most effective.

Initially, organizations often place most of their attention on the source group, concentrating on *who* has the knowledge within the organization and identifying *what* knowledge they have that would prove useful to transfer. The tendency is to give less attention to the characteristics of the teams that will be the recipients of the knowledge. Before selecting a transfer mechanism, it is important to find answers to these questions:

> How similar are the task and the context of the receiving team(s) to those of the source team?

> Does the receiving team(s) have the absorptive capacity (experience, technical knowledge, and shared language) to implement what the source team has developed?

THE NATURE OF THE TASK

A second factor that impacts transfer effectiveness is the nature of the task. Some tasks are repeated daily, even hourly, on a job. Other tasks occur infrequently or only in some unusual set of circumstances—for example, a part breaks that has never broken before, or a machine turns up that is so old only someone with a twenty-year history in the organization remembers how to deal with it.

Some jobs consist of parts that are done the same way every time and other parts that are different every time they occur (such jobs are termed *nonroutine*). The job of a copy machine repair technician, for example, has both routine and nonroutine aspects. Diagnosing what is wrong with a copy machine, it turns out, is a nonroutine task—it is like detective work. When the repair technician arrives on the scene to fix the copier, the machine operator may have a lot to tell about what has gone wrong, what happened right before the machine broke, what has happened in the past, and so on. The repair technician has to ferret out the relevant from the nonrelevant parts of this often lengthy story. The technician adds to that information the results of several diagnostic tests and may even check through the wastebasket for "the mistakes." All the while the technician is trying to pacify an irritated and rushed machine operator who is anxious to get on with the copying. In any particular situation what the technician does next is emergent, not linear—a very nonroutine task.

On the other hand, replacing parts is a routine aspect of the repair technician's job. Once the diagnosis is made, fixing the machine, cleaning the machine, and doing preventive maintenance are routine tasks. Whether a task is routine or nonroutine impacts what kind of system would transfer knowledge most effectively.

The questions to ask about the nature of the task are:

How frequently does this task occur? Daily? Monthly? Yearly?

Is the task routine or nonroutine? Are there clear, fixed steps or is each step variable?

THE TYPE OF KNOWLEDGE THAT IS BEING TRANSFERRED

Finally, the type of knowledge that is being transferred makes a difference in what method of transfer works best. Think of type of knowledge as a continuum from explicit to tacit. At one end of the continuum is knowledge that can be laid out in procedures, steps, and standards—explicit knowledge. It can be translated into checklists and specifications. At the other end of the continuum is knowledge that is primarily in the heads of people—tacit knowledge.

We recognize as tacit the knowledge that allows an outstanding medical diagnostician to hit the mark, although she may have difficulty saying exactly how she knew what was wrong with the patient. We commend the skilled salesman who knows just the right moment to close a sale, although he may not be able to explain to the sales trainee why then and not five minutes later. We often think of the knowledge of these "masters" of their craft as largely intuition. But cognitive scientists would assure us that tacit knowledge is very real, even if it is difficult to capture in documents or even in spoken words.[5] Consider the way a novice chef like me cooks by following a cookbook (using explicit knowledge) compared to the way a master chef cooks (using tacit knowledge). The chef knows when the bread is at just the right level of elasticity because of the way it feels.

I know the bread is ready because I have kneaded it for the requisite twenty minutes.

Michael Polanyi, the distinguished chemist and philosopher, was one of the first theorists to talk about these two types of knowledge. He explains tacit knowledge as "we can know more than we can tell," and uses a familiar example to illustrate this knowing: our almost infallible ability to recognize a human face, versus our inadequate attempts to describe in words what that recognition entails.[6] His illustration reminds us that everyone has the capability to use tacit knowledge. Thus tacit knowledge is not just about the difference between what experts know and what beginners know, although experts do have more tacit knowledge about their subject than do beginners. All of us possess and use both tacit and explicit knowledge, although some tasks make greater use of one than the other.

Polanyi describes tacit knowledge as being "in-dwelling," meaning that it is constructed from our experience in the world—the sense we make of what we see, touch, feel, and hear. He does not view tacit and explicit as two different kinds of knowing, but rather sees tacit knowledge as undergirding all explicit knowledge. And although I have been talking about knowledge as either tacit or explicit, I too recognize that most knowledge, particularly the common knowledge in organizations, has components that are both tacit and explicit. Thus most knowledge learned from experience in organizations does not fall on either extreme end of the continuum but rather is a combination or falls at some more intermediate position.

We often think of explicit knowledge, or that part of knowledge that is explicit, as being easier to transfer than tacit knowledge. I am not sure that is so, but I am sure it requires different transfer processes than tacit knowledge does. In chapters 5 and 6, I describe some of the innovative processes that organizations have devised to transfer tacit knowledge.

Another factor to consider in terms of type of knowledge is how many different functional areas of the organization are impacted by the knowledge that is being transferred. Does the knowledge impact the work of only one individual? A whole team? Multiple divisions? The more cross-functional the intended impact, the more complex the knowledge. For example,

General Motors (GM) created a joint venture with Toyota, the NUMMI (New United Motor Manufacturing, Inc.) plant, in order to bring into GM the knowledge that Toyota had developed in Japan. After the NUMMI plant was up and running in the United States, GM brought hundreds of study teams from its other plants to NUMMI in the hope of transferring to them what had been learned at NUMMI. These efforts were largely unsuccessful, in part because of the enormous level of complexity of the knowledge embedded in the NUMMI plant. To make use of this knowledge, every department and unit of a recipient plant would have needed to gain new knowledge. And they would have needed to learn as well all the interactions between the units—what authors Geary Rummler and Alan Brache call the "white spaces."[7] Even if the knowledge within each unit were explicit enough to be written down (which would be difficult), the relationships between units might still be largely tacit. Contrast the NUMMI example with a team in Atlanta that finds a quicker way to install the front bumper on a car and is able to transfer that knowledge to a team that works in a plant in Kansas City. The scope of knowledge is clearly narrower, less complex, and of course explicit.

The type of knowledge then, whether it is tacit or explicit, and the scope of the knowledge are important factors in how knowledge is transferred. The questions to be asked are:

> Is the knowledge of the source team primarily tacit or explicit?

> How many functional areas of the organization will be impacted by implementing the knowledge? One team? One division? The whole organization?

CHOOSING THE MOST EFFECTIVE WAY TO TRANSFER KNOWLEDGE

I have used these criteria—who the intended receiver is, the nature of the task, and the type of knowledge to be transferred—to develop five categories of knowledge transfer, each of which requires different design elements to make the transfer successful. In the following chapters I describe organizational examples that fit into each of these five categories. Following the examples I identify the design principles that facilitate that kind of transfer. The five categories are outlined briefly here.

The first category, *Serial Transfer*, applies to a team that does a task and then the same team repeats the task in a new context. An example is Bechtel's steam generator replacement team. This team replaces a generator at a specific site, perhaps in a chemical plant, working over a period of two to three months. When the team has completed the task, it moves on to, perhaps, a refinery, to replace a generator. There the team reuses the knowledge it gained from its work at the chemical plant. In Serial Transfer, the source team and the receiving team are one and the same. Serial Transfer offers a way to prevent the repetition of costly mistakes and to increase efficiencies of speed and quality.

The second category, *Near Transfer*, involves transferring knowledge from a source team to a receiving team that is doing a similar task in a similar context but in a different location. The task involves largely routine work that the team engages in repeatedly. An example is a team at the Ford plant in Chicago that is able to reduce the amount of time it takes to install front brakes by fifteen seconds by using a best practice generated in Atlanta. Near Transfer moves explicit knowledge from location to location. As many companies have discovered, the potential for cost savings in transferring best practice is enormous.

The third category, *Far Transfer*, involves transferring tacit knowledge from a source team to a receiving team when the knowledge is about a nonroutine task. An example is a team of peers that is invited to meet with an oil exploration team to assist in the interpretation of data the receiving team has collected. The knowledge to be transferred is primarily in the heads of the visiting team members, certainly not written down as steps or sequences. Because the interpretation of seismic or geological data is a task that is emergent and variable, those who hold the knowledge must themselves be immersed in the situation to draw on and transfer what they know. Far Transfer makes possible the leveraging of people who have very specialized and critical knowledge. It provides a way to apply those knowledge resources to costly decisions and problems.

The fourth category, *Strategic Transfer*, involves transferring very complex knowledge, such as how to launch a product or make an acquisition, from one team to another in cases where the teams may be separated by both time and space. This transfer differs from Far Transfer in that the implementation of the transferred knowledge impacts large parts of the system, whereas Far Transfer is more limited in scope, often impacting only one team or unit. The cross-functional team that is the source will have gained important knowledge that could save dollars and effort the next time around—if the knowledge can be transferred. Using acquisition as an example, the receiving team may be responsible for acquiring a company that is larger, less friendly, and located in a different part of the world than the company the source team was dealing with—an entirely different context. Yet some part of the source team's knowledge, tacit and explicit, will be valuable in the new situation. The knowledge that the receiving team puts to use will impact many different functional areas. Strategic Transfer is both very complex and very vital, and there is no way that the simple transfer systems of "best practice" can accomplish such a task. In chapter 6, I describe how organizations are building effective Strategic Transfer systems that prevent them from having to reinvent the wheel and repeat costly mistakes year after year.

The fifth category, *Expert Transfer*, involves transferring explicit knowledge about a task that may be done infrequently. An example is a technician who e-mails his network to ask how to increase the brightness on an out-of-date monitor and gets back explicit knowledge that allows his team to complete its task in a timely manner. Again the question is how to leverage costly or scarce human resources. But in the case of Expert Transfer, because the needed expertise can be offered in a formula or a procedure, the problem does not have to be interpreted, only clearly stated.

SUMMARY

Organizations need to balance two important kinds of knowledge activities: (1) creating new common knowledge, and (2) leveraging common knowledge across organizational boundaries. Both activities have always occurred in organizations to some extent, but often as informal or ad hoc processes. As awareness of the importance of organizational knowledge grows, organizations are seeking ways to address both in a more deliberate and systematic manner.

Many organizations that have been on the leading edge of knowledge management activities have demonstrated the tremendous cost savings that can be achieved through sharing knowledge. But other early users have found that unless the transfer system is an appropriate fit for the kind of knowledge and task, it may end up being ignored and eventually abandoned.

In the next chapter I describe the first of the five transfer processes that offer a more systematic approach to building knowledge transfer systems.

CHAPTER 3

SERIAL TRANSFER

One task of the U.S. Army troops that arrived in Haiti in 1994 was to remove guns and ammunition from the many rebel towns. After the first attempt, the unit assigned to do this held an After Action Review (AAR) to assess what had happened in order to improve the next attempt. During the meeting the soldiers recognized that their effort to disarm the town had been met with considerable resistance. One soldier noted that he had observed few dogs in the town. Someone else had noticed that the Haitians were fearful of the large German Shepherds that were used by the military police. That led a third person to suggest that the unit borrow some dogs from the military police so that in disarming the next town they could use the dogs out front with the hope of reducing the resistance.

After the next, and more successful, attempt to disarm a town, an AAR was again held and yielded additional ideas. In this AAR it was noted that the villagers were more cooperative when in their homes than when they were in the street. So in disarming the third town it was decided that most of the interaction should be held within the homes of the villagers. The next AAR produced yet other useful suggestion based on the observation that the Haitians were particularly respectful to women. The group decided to put a woman in charge of the team and to display particular deference to her in front of the Haitians, again as a way to more effectively and efficiently accomplish their mission.[1]

The Serial Transfer system involves transferring the knowledge a team has learned from doing its task in one setting to the next time that team does the task in a different setting. The repeated action and the knowledge gained from each action happen in a serial fashion.[2] The knowledge that the team gained during the first experience helps it to function more effectively the next time. But for that to happen, knowledge has to be transferred from individual team members to the team as a whole.

When a team is engaged in a task, (e.g., drilling a well, developing a product, delivering a performance) each member of the team takes away from the experience a number of observations, among them:

- what actions the individual team member took (the term "actions" here includes what the person did physically, what the person said, what the person refrained from doing, etc.),

- how that team member's actions impacted the outcome,

- what the team member noted about the actions that other team members took,

- how the team member was impacted by the actions of other team members,

- how the actions of other team members impacted the outcome,

- what occurred in the environment, both expected and unexpected, and

- the impact of the environment on the team member and on other team members.

All of these observations, and more, are held in the mind of each team member and are necessarily unique to each team member. Each team member can use the personal understanding gained from the experience to plan what to do differently during the next action. However, a team's action is more than the sum of individual parts. So for a team to perform more effectively the next time it takes the same action, much of what each team member has learned from the experience must be made available to others.

Serial Transfer is a process that moves the unique knowledge that each individual has constructed into a group or public space so that the knowledge can be integrated and made sense of by the whole team.[3] But the transfer process is more complex than just team members reporting out their knowledge so that others in the group are aware of it. Individual team members are able to use what others have said to reinterpret how they themselves understand the situation. In the Haiti example, the soldier who "knew" that he had not seen many dogs in the village now "knows" that in a new way. The fact has not changed, but the way that fact relates to other facts has changed. This integration of ideas spawns the reconsideration of cause and effect, it produces the if/then that leads to new team action, it identifies discrepancies in the perception of what occurred, and it develops new generalizations that may guide future action. It is in this important sense that a transfer of knowledge has occurred, from individual knowing to group knowing.

The whole team can then act on its shared knowledge the next time it takes action. The team may, of course, choose to change very little from its previous actions, particularly if the overall action was successful. Or the team may realize that it needs to alter a few of the actions of particular members or take an entirely new action in order to reach its goals. Figure 3–1 shows how the translation of experience into knowledge includes individual-to-group transfer.

It turns out that experience is a poor teacher because it requires interpretation of what are often confusing facts and events.[4] The relationship between cause and effect is often quite complex. Experience relies heavily on human memory, which is

FIGURE 3-1

TRANSFERRING MEMBER KNOWLEDGE TO TEAM KNOWLEDGE

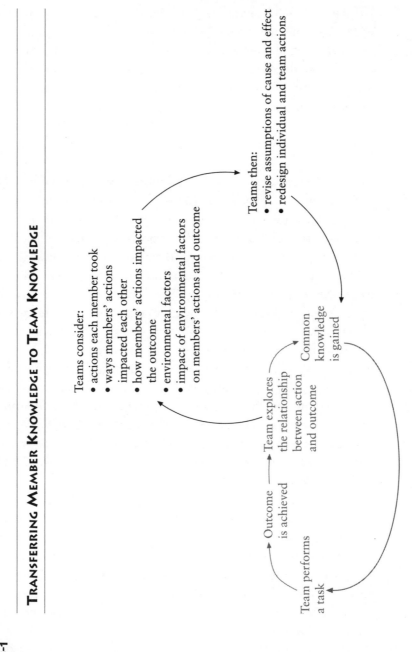

Team performs a task

Outcome is achieved

Team explores the relationship between action and outcome

Common knowledge is gained

Teams consider:
- actions each member took
- ways members' actions impacted each other
- how members' actions impacted the outcome
- environmental factors
- impact of environmental factors on members' actions and outcome

Teams then:
- revise assumptions of cause and effect
- redesign individual and team actions

notoriously fallible. Moreover, most of the outcomes a team accomplishes have multiple causes, not just one, and teasing those causal relationships out of the experiences of ten or fifteen team members is a problematic task. The most functional way to deal with these barriers to creating useful and valid knowledge from experience is to use the checks and balances that multiple perspectives provide, especially when they are offered in the spirit of learning.

A team can, of course, leave the task of interpretation to the leader or to a member who is judged to be most expert. But when the available knowledge about actions and outcomes is distributed across team members, expertise does not result in drawing more accurate relationships between actions and outcomes. Expertise provides necessary input, but the relationships between actions and outcomes are more accurately drawn by a group that can correct, support, and build on each other's insights.

EXAMPLES OF SERIAL TRANSFER

Three examples of Serial Transfer follow. The first is the U.S. Army using the After Action Review process described at the beginning of this chapter. The second is British Petroleum, which has modeled its system on the Army, and the third is Bechtel's Steam Generator Replacement Group.

U.S. ARMY—AFTER ACTION REVIEW

Probably the best-known example of leveraging knowledge within a team is the U.S. Army's use of After Action Reviews. The AARs are held at the end of any team or unit action with the intent of reusing what has been learned immediately in the next battle or project. These brief meetings are attended by everyone who was engaged in the effort, regardless of rank. The Army's simple guidelines for conducting AARs are (1) no sugar coating, (2) discover ground truth, (3) no thin skins, (4) take notes, and (5) call it like you see it. The meetings are facilitated by someone in the unit, sometimes the ranking officer but just as often another member of the team. The learning from these meetings is captured both by the members, who all write and keep personal notes about what they need to do differently, and by the facilitator, who captures on a flip chart or chalkboard what the unit as a whole determines that it needs to do differently in the next engagement. Army After Action Reviews have standardized three key questions: What was supposed to happen?, What happened?, and What accounts for the difference? An AAR may last fifteen minutes or an hour depending on the action that is being discussed, but in any case, it is not a lengthy meeting.

Interestingly, AARs had their beginnings in training simulations as a way for a team that was engaged in a mock battle to gain as much learning as possible from the training event. However, AARs proved so useful to a team's effectiveness that gradually they began to be used in nontraining situations as well. Today, they have spread throughout the Army, not because someone at the top of the military hierarchy has required their use, but because the troops find them helpful in getting the job done. The first peacekeeping troops in Haiti in 1994 provide a useful illustration of how AARs can improve a team's next action.

It will probably not surprise anyone that the soldiers offered useful ideas that made the next action more effective. However, what makes AARs beneficial is that this kind of collective knowledge pooling occurs not just once but over and over again. The speed, regularity, and discipline with which AARs are held in the U.S. Army are the factors of most interest.

British Petroleum—AARs

Borrowing the AAR from the U.S. Army, British Petroleum has made it the middle step of its three-part knowledge management process. BP calls its practice of AAR "learning during" and, along with "learning before" and "learning after" (more about these later), has built a set of knowledge management practices that it implements in a systematic way. The idea of an AAR is so uncomplicated that it takes little instruction to accomplish. BP has designed a simple, one-page flyer that explains what an AAR is, where it came from, and how to do it. That basic explanation has been adequate to enable units in the field to implement the practice on their own.

The questions BP asks in an AAR are the same ones the U.S. Army uses, although the answers are, of course, very different. For example, the question "What was supposed to happen?" might yield, "We were supposed to install the new pump by the end of the shutdown period." Many projects in the oil industry take several months to complete, so AARs are held along the way, at the end of any "event" that has a definable beginning and end. During the course of a lengthy project, a BP team may hold, and benefit from, ten to fifteen AARs. On development wells, where teams often work around the clock, two AARs may be held each day, one for each shift. BP has found that if the team waits until the well is in to hold the AAR, much of the knowledge is lost. After a few days team members have forgotten what happened and, more important, the reasons for their actions. The only way to translate the experience of bringing in a well into knowledge that can be used on site for the next well is to hold frequent AARs.

BECHTEL—LESSONS LEARNED MEETINGS

Bechtel's Steam Generator Replacement Group also uses this practice, although it calls the meetings "lessons learned" instead of AARs. Bechtel is a multibillion-dollar international engineering, procurement, and construction company engaged in large-scale projects, such as power plants, petrochemical facilities, airports, mining facilities, and major infrastructure projects. Unlike other parts of Bechtel in which individuals work in ever-changing project teams, the Steam Generator Replacement Group is a small specialized unit that works on a lot of jobs together. Anything learned on one job can be immediately used by the team on the next job. The nature of its work leaves little room for error. The average window of time to replace a steam generator is seventy days or less, unlike the typical Bechtel project, which may last two years or more. This unforgiving schedule mandates that the Steam Generator Replacement Group learn from its own lessons, because even a small mistake can result in a significant delay to a project. The lessons are captured in two ways: first, in weekly meetings to which supervisors are required to bring lessons learned; then, at the end of each project, the project manager brings all players together for a full day to focus on the lessons learned.

The next section spells out what an organization needs to put into place in order to have an effective system for Serial Transfer. First, I apply the three criteria for selection of a transfer process to one of the examples; then I outline the design principles based on them.

CRITERIA RELATED TO SERIAL TRANSFER

The three criteria that I described in chapter 2 are presented here with the questions a designer or design team of a knowledge transfer system needs to ask in order to determine which of the five transfer systems will be most effective. Having made that determination, the designer would apply the appropriate design guidelines.

To illustrate the way the criteria can be used, I am going to do a bit of reverse engineering. Rather than apply the criteria to a fictional organization, I use the Bechtel Steam Generator Replacement Group, and pose the criteria questions (left-hand column) as though this team had determined that it should transfer the knowledge it gains from one action to its next action. The way that Bechtel would answer the questions regarding the knowledge it wants to transfer (right-hand column) leads to the conclusion that the most effective transfer process would be Serial Transfer. It would, therefore, in this reverse-engineered example, design a system based on the Serial Transfer guidelines outlined below.

1. Who the intended receiver of the knowledge is in terms of similarity of task and context

QUESTIONS	ANSWERS FOR BECHTEL STEAM GENERATOR REPLACEMENT GROUP
How similar are the task and the context of	The task is similar for the Steam Generator Replacement Group because

the receiving team(s) to those of the source team?

the knowledge is put to use by the same Group that generated it. However, the context changes with each new site.

Does the receiving team(s) have the absorptive capacity (experience, technical knowledge, shared language) to implement what the source team has developed?

The Steam Generator Replacement Group has the absorptive capacity because it builds its own knowledge base as it goes along.

2. How routine and frequent the task is

QUESTIONS	ANSWERS FOR BECHTEL STEAM GENERATOR REPLACEMENT GROUP
How frequently does this task occur? Daily? Monthly? Yearly?	The Steam Generator Replacement Group repeats its task every two to three months.
Is the task routine or nonroutine? Are there clear steps, or is each next step variable?	The Steam Generator Replacement Group's task has some routine elements. But it also has many nonroutine elements because each time it works at a new site it faces differences in size, age of equipment, contract agreements, legal issues, and so on. That makes each next step variable.

3. The kind of knowledge that is being transferred

QUESTIONS	ANSWERS FOR BECHTEL STEAM GENERATOR REPLACEMENT GROUP
Is the knowledge of the source team primarily tacit or explicit?	The knowledge that the Steam Generator Replacement Group transfers from one site to another is both tacit and explicit. The explicit parts can be written into procedures and regulations; the tacit parts must be constructed from the memory of team

members as they address the new situation. In discussing the lessons learned from a just-completed project, the team members make their tacit knowledge explicit both to themselves and to other team members.

| How many functional areas of the organization will be impacted by implementing the knowledge? One team? One division? The whole organization? | Although an entire plant is impacted by the speed with which the Steam Generator Replacement Group accomplishes its task, only the team itself is impacted by the knowledge it gains at one site and reuses at the next. |

DESIGN GUIDELINES

Because the design guidelines that follow relate only to Serial Transfer, rather than to the many other possible "end-of" meetings that go on in organizations, I first want to differentiate Serial Transfer meetings from all-purpose debriefing techniques. For example, the familiar end-of-training evaluation meeting where participants are asked to offer the instructor ideas to improve the course is not Serial Transfer because those offering the ideas are not themselves responsible for changing the course. Only the instructors can act on the knowledge generated. End-of-course discussions then, as useful as they may be, don't meet the condition that those who generate the knowledge must also be those who can act on it.

Another necessary condition of Serial Transfer is that team members are interdependent and working together toward an agreed-upon goal. Many teams are a team in name only; they are really a group of individual contributors who all happen to do the same type of work (perhaps for the same manager) but who do not depend on each other to get that work done. Such groups may benefit from occasional team meetings, but they are not engaging in Serial Transfer. But when the situation is one in which each member's effectiveness depends on the effectiveness of the other members, then Serial Transfer can work to increase the team's productivity.

Given those conditions the following guidelines create effective Serial Transfer.

MEETINGS ARE HELD REGULARLY

It is the discipline of the regularity of these meetings that makes them effective. Serial Transfer meetings are held either at a scheduled time (e.g., every morning or every week) or at the end of a defined action. In either case they are not "called" meetings whose purpose is to address an exception, such as a problem that has occurred, or indeed even because a success was achieved. Rather they are a part of the way the work of the team gets accomplished—a work routine. To some extent the regularity also can reduce team members' anxiety that the meeting will be about placing blame—a concern that arises when meetings are held only after something has gone wrong.

MEETINGS ARE BRIEF

Perhaps because of their regularity, Serial Transfer meetings are quick and to the point. At Bio-Tek Instruments they are called "standing meetings"—everyone stands rather than sits—as a kind of tacit assurance that the meeting will be short. Even "boring" meetings are tolerable if they last only twenty minutes.

In order to be brief, the meetings have to have a recognized format—a clarity about what is on the table and what should be left to other kinds of meetings. The three questions the U.S. Army uses, for example, provide that kind of format:

- What was supposed to happen?

- What happened?

- What accounts for the difference?

EVERYONE INVOLVED IN THE ACTION PARTICIPATES IN THE MEETING

This is an important guideline of Serial Transfer for two reasons. First, the information and ideas of everyone are necessary to get a full picture; someone may well have seen or been aware of something that others did not see. Second, the attendance of everyone is evidence of shared responsibility. Not to attend is a tacit statement that "The results were none of my doing," as in "I just give the orders" or "I just do what I'm told." No one is so unimportant as not to share responsibility for what happened and for making it happen more effectively the next time. And no one is so important as not to need the insights of others.

THERE ARE NO RECRIMINATIONS

The Army has a very clear rule: Nothing said in an AAR can be used in any kind of personnel action. It is a hard rule to believe in, but a necessary one if people are to tell the truth, or at least their version of the truth, in the meetings. However, team members don't believe it just because someone says, "Speak your mind and there will be no recriminations." The only way that rule becomes believable is when some courageous team member says something like "What we lacked in this situation was clear leadership," and then waits for the response. If the response is a threat or a putdown, then others see that they can't trust the rule. If the response is lighthearted or an acknowledgment of fault by the leader, then others can begin to believe the rule. "No recriminations" is a rule that has to be experienced to be believed. But teams do not have to start with believability; it can grow over time.

Because the intent of these meetings is to understand more fully what happened and what needs to be done differently the next time, they are more descriptive than evaluative. But that does not lessen the need to "call it like you see it."

REPORTS ARE NOT FORWARDED

In many of these meetings no written record is kept. In others notes are taken but retained only for local use and distribution.

At BP an administrative assistant may write up the notes from an AAR, but those notes are for the team's own use and review, and are not forwarded to any higher level. Likewise in the U.S. Army, the notes are for local use. In special situations in the Army, the AAR notes are asked to be sent to the Center for Army Lessons Learned (CALL) if, for example, Army officials have identified the area that unit is working in as one in which knowledge is needed for the whole (e.g., how to build a bridge in a particular type of terrain or how to achieve better cooperation between two branches of the service). But even under these special conditions the AAR notes are not sent through a reporting line but through a "knowledge line." More typically, notes from an AAR stay in the unit.

The policy of not forwarding reports up the organizational ladder or even laterally across the organization is a critical element in Serial Transfer. It avoids many of the concerns and fears that teams have about meeting to review their actions—concerns about "not wanting to air their dirty laundry" or that they will gain a bad reputation with others in the company. If a team is going to learn, it needs to be able to try out actions that may not work perfectly the first time, to thoroughly analyze those actions, to acknowledge misjudgments, and to find ways to move forward. That is much easier and safer to do when the discussion stays with the group that is working on the problem.

This idea may seem contrary to the notion that teams can and should learn from other teams. However, the key to successful transfer of knowledge is knowing under what circumstances different types of knowledge can be shared. What a team learns from its repeated actions and reflections on those actions may well be shared at some later time, but it is not effective to do so through sharing the reports of each successive meeting.

MEETINGS ARE FACILITATED LOCALLY

Serial Transfer meetings are facilitated by a member of the team. The responsibility of the facilitator is to remind the group of the simple guidelines and to keeps the discussion focused on the few critical questions. After repeated meetings the responsibility may become almost perfunctory. The facilitator role may rotate among members or may be taken by someone in the group who is recognized as having particularly good facilitation skills.

Local facilitation means that outside expertise is not required in order to hold a Serial Transfer meeting. The rules and guidelines are few and easily understood by everyone. Using local facilitators makes possible both the regularity and frequency of the meetings, as well as justifying the short duration. It would hardly be cost effective to bring in an outside consultant to run a fifteen-minute meeting.

BUSINESS DRIVER

The business driver for Serial Transfer is improvement in the team's outcome measures. That could be a way to get a task that is repeated accomplished quicker, at lower cost, with higher quality, or with more satisfied customers. The way Serial Transfer gets the team to that goal is by carefully examining the relationship between the actions of members and the outcomes they have achieved.

BARRIERS AND PROBLEMS

In this section I address some of the concerns that people raise when I talk about making Serial Transfer work.

TEAM MEMBERS WON'T TAKE THE TIME TO MEET

Team members have no reason to meet at the end of a project unless the meeting accomplishes something they value. For the teams that employ Serial Transfer what is valued is reaching an identified goal. The goal is evident in the Army example, where life or death is a likely consequence of action. Likewise, the need to reduce the number of days that a generator is down is apparent to Bechtel's Steam Generator Replacement Group. BP establishes a best-in-class number for each step of the drilling process that the team tracks itself against. In each case AARs provide assistance in getting to the identified target.

In translating experience into knowledge (see figure 3–1), which is what Serial Transfer does, being aware of the outcome is the second step. Team members cannot develop knowledge about the relationship between action and outcome if the outcome is unknown or, more accurately, if the outcome is unknown to those who are trying to construct the knowledge. A "known" outcome does not necessarily mean numbers or measures (e.g., soldiers know the outcome if they have taken the hill), but for most organizational purposes, measures are a useful way to track progress toward a goal. Figure 3–2 shows how an identified target and outcome measures fit into the knowledge transfer picture.

For constructing knowledge, who "owns" the measures is a critical factor in their use. Team members "own" the measures that they themselves establish, track, and report.[5] Moreover, these measures are primarily for their own use rather than serving as a reporting mechanism. There may well be end goal measures that are reported up through the organization, but the day-to-day measures that help the team continuously improve its task are not reported. It is difficult for the same set of numbers to serve both improvement and reporting functions; difficult, because if team members knew that the measures they were using to identify errors and problems in the team's processes were to be reported upward, they would be more likely to design measures that give a favorable impression rather than a useful assessment. Serial Transfer requires that team members make mistakes together and clean up the mess together without recriminations from above. The measures they own help teams identify their mistakes.

Team Members Lack the Skills to Have Knowledge-Producing Conversations

When the type of knowledge being developed is on the explicit end of the explicit/tacit continuum, as in the Army and the BP drilling examples, few skills beyond normal communication skills are needed to translate experience into common knowledge. Having in place (1) a standardized format of questions, (2) a member of the team who serves as facilitator and who is

FIGURE 3-2

How Outcome Measures Facilitate the Construction of Common Knowledge

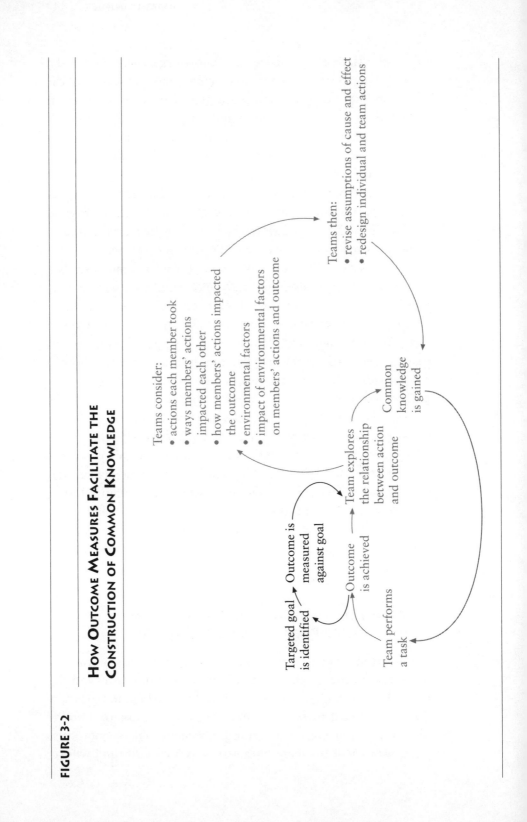

familiar with the process, (3) basic norms of truth telling, and (4) a no-recriminations policy is sufficient for Serial Transfer.

However, as the complexity of the knowledge increases, moving toward the tacit end of the continuum, a greater level of skill may be needed. Training team members in the communication skills of advocacy and inquiry can assist them in learning to provide the reasoning behind their conclusions, to examine their own assumptions, to inquire into the assumptions of others, and to remain open to errors in their own reasoning. This set of skills, which behavioral scientist and business communication theorist Chris Argyris calls Model II, has long been associated with organizational learning and is a proven way to deal with the fallibility of human memory and the tendency to draw inferences based on scant data.[6]

TEAM MEMBERS DISPERSE BEFORE THE END OF THE PROJECT

For projects that last over months, team members may come and go, moving on to other projects when they have made their contributions. So by the end of the project, team members may have dispersed across the organization and be fully engaged in new efforts. In this configuration, the same team does not do the next project together; rather, a new team is formed for each project. This situation is, of course, not Serial Transfer because the same team is not able to transfer its knowledge to the next site. It is, however, still possible for the organization to benefit from any Serial Transfer meetings in the following way.

Imagine each source team member carrying a suitcase of knowledge to the next team. Each suitcase is filled with the knowledge that team member drew out of his or her experience with the source team. If the source team held frequent Serial Transfer meetings to construct knowledge from its experience, then the suitcase that each team member takes to the next team is filled not only with his or her own knowledge, but with additional and more fully tested common knowledge developed in the Serial Transfer meetings. Each member's knowledge has been tested against the perceptions of others and in the process has been both corrected and enlarged.

THE TEAM IS VIRTUAL

Serial Transfer works the same way with virtual teams as it does with face-to-face teams. It is, however, important that the same design guidelines be in place. Meetings should be:

- held regularly,
- brief, with a set of standard questions or elements,
- participated in by everyone involved in the action, and
- facilitated locally.

BP, for example, has invested heavily in the hardware and software to support its virtual teams, including desktop PCs equipped with videoconferencing capability and groupware. The company's initial pilot project for virtual teamwork also had a heavy involvement of behavioral scientists, who helped team members learn to work effectively in a virtual environment. BP has been remarkably successful in accomplishing Serial Transfer in a virtual environment. An offshore exploration team, for example, may be made up of members who are out on the rig and others who are onshore. Morning meetings are frequently held between these two groups using videoconferencing. These virtual meetings have reduced the person-hours needed to solve problems between the land-based engineers and the offshore rig crews as well as decreased the number of helicopter trips to the offshore platforms. BP estimates that the videoconferencing system alone has produced a cost savings of over $30 million in its first year of operation.

SUMMARY

Holding a team meeting to reflect on what has happened is certainly not new to organizations. The medical profession has a long tradition of holding "postmortems" when an unexpected death occurs. Safety organizations have often debriefed after a disaster or a near miss to find out what went wrong. But the meeting of team members for the purpose of constructing knowledge out of their experience *is* a relatively new way to think about such meetings.

TABLE 3-1

DESIGN GUIDELINES FOR SERIAL TRANSFER

Definition	The knowledge a team has gained from doing its task in one setting is transferred to the next time that team does the task in a different setting.
Similarity of task and context	The receiving team (which is also the source team) does a similar task in a new context.
Nature of the task	Frequent and nonroutine
Type of knowledge	Tacit and explicit
Design guidelines	Meetings are held regularly
	Meetings are brief
	Everyone involved in the action participates in the meeting
	There are no recriminations
	Reports are not forwarded
	Meetings are facilitated locally
Example	A power generator replacement team replaces a generator in a chemical plant. The team uses that knowledge when replacing a generator in a refinery.

Serial Transfer places the focus on collective knowledge rather than individual knowledge. It assumes the capability of team members to construct knowledge themselves, rather than simply providing data or input for others to use. It focuses on the complexity of the relationship between action and outcome and assumes that team members can add a valuable perspective that helps make that relationship more accurate. This intentional effort to translate experience into common knowledge is an outgrowth of organizations' increasingly seeing themselves as knowledge intensive and viewing their employees as knowledge workers.

Table 3–1 lists all of the design guidelines for Serial Transfer in an abbreviated form as well as listing the transfer criteria. In describing each of the other four transfer methods I also provide a table, and in chapter 8, I combine all these tables into one in order to reveal the major characteristics of each category and also highlight the differences between categories. The differences are significant because they determine which type of transfer system an organization may implement most effectively.

In chapter 4, I turn to the second transfer type, Near Transfer. Again I have provided some examples and the guidelines that make this kind of transfer effective.

CHAPTER 4

NEAR
TRANSFER

Jack Ruden is the Focal Point for Vehicle Operations at a Ford plant in the Midwest. Vehicle Operations is where the final assembly is done—the car is put together. As the Focal Point he is supposed to check into the company Intranet once a week to see what new Best Practices have appeared. When he checks in this morning, five new practices are there, all of them practices that have been implemented in other Vehicle Operations plants. He looks through them and notes that a couple are things that his plant cannot use, but one he thinks might be really viable. The report says that an automated "alcohol wipe" was entered by the Atlanta plant, that the equipment costs $40,000, and that it saved the Atlanta plant 0.4 of a person in labor, which could then be redeployed. It also increased the plant's quality level because before that the wipe was done by the person who applied the roof molding and that person didn't always wipe it adequately. If the alcohol wipe wasn't done properly, the seal some-

times didn't hold. On Jack's computer screen is a picture of the automated equipment that does the alcohol wipe. Jack prints off a copy of the picture and the report and takes it around to a couple of supervisors in the area that wipes the molding to see what they think. The supervisors think it is worth looking into. Jack calls the supplier, who is listed in the Best Practices report, and gets more information. He will take the idea to the next meeting of the plant management committee, to see if the committee wants to make the investment. Jack knows that it is likely that committee members will want to move forward because new practice will help them make their "task." Each plant is "tasked" by corporate to make a 5 percent improvement in productivity each year. Most of that improvement will come from savings in redeploying labor to areas of the plant that need more help, although it could also come from materials or energy. So the savings of 0.4 of a person in labor would go a long way in helping the plant make its "task." After the management meeting, Jack will go back onto the Intranet and report the disposition he has made of each of the Best Practices that have appeared. Next to this one he will check "adopted" and record a projection of value to his plant. Later, when the equipment is in place, he will also enter the cost and the amount of actual savings his plant achieved. Other Best Practices that have appeared on his screen he may mark as under investigation, previously adopted, not applicable, or too costly for this site.

Near Transfer is applicable when a team has learned something from its experience that the organization would like to replicate in other teams that are doing very similar work. I call this Near Transfer not because of the geography involved but because of the similarity between the source team and the receiving team. Learning theorists have long known that the more a learning experience resembles the place and situation where the knowledge will be used on the job, the more effective the transfer of learning.[1] They refer to this similarity as *near transfer,* so I have borrowed the term to describe knowledge transfer that occurs between two very similar teams that may, however, be located in different parts of the world.

The stage is set for Near Transfer when a team has developed some knowledge about how to do its task more effectively or efficiently—it has, in effect, created the common knowledge described in chapter 3. Moreover, it has put that knowledge to use and has shown that it produces results. The common knowledge may be as simple as finding a new piece of equipment that reduces labor costs, as the Ford story illustrates. Or it may entail a more complex procedure or series of steps that improve effectiveness, as some of the later examples in this chapter illustrate.

In many organizations this kind of improvement is thought of as "best practice." Since the beginning of the quality movement, organizations have been able to effectively identify best practice, but the goal of transferring that practice to other parts of the organization has remained a stumbling block.[2] Recently, with the emphasis on knowledge management, organizations have begun to find effective ways to accomplish this elusive goal. In the examples below, Ford, Texas Instruments, and Ernst & Young all employ very different processes for Near Transfer, but it is possible to identify, within the differences, the basic guidelines that make the process work.

EXAMPLES OF NEAR TRANSFER

FORD—BEST PRACTICE REPLICATION

Ford's Best Practice Replication was initiated in the Vehicle Operations division, which is composed of thirty-seven plants where vehicles are assembled and painted. Each week, the Focal Point in each plant receives over the Intranet five to eight best practices that apply only to Vehicle Operations plants. Focal Points are production engineers appointed by each plant manager to be responsible for best practices; in some plants there may be as many as three Focal Points, each of whom functions in a different area (e.g. Paint, Assembly, or Stamping). The Focal Point is responsible both for retrieving the best practices that are "pushed" to the plants and for entering best practices from his or her own plant into the system.

The report page on the Intranet is concise and standardized.

It includes where the idea originated, a brief description of the practice, the savings it achieved, and the name and phone number of a contact from whom to obtain more information. The page usually has a picture, and soon video will be added because the Focal Points have found that many best practices require seeing the motion involved in order to adequately understand them. The Focal Point is required to mark a scorecard that is attached to each best practice that appears on the monitor, using one of several choices: adopted, under investigation, previously adopted, not applicable, or too costly. None of the plants is required to adopt any best practice that appears on the Web site, but the Focal Point does have to respond to each.

Once a best practice has been adopted in a plant, the Focal Point is responsible for reporting the cost involved and the actual savings achieved. The Focal Points have considerable confidence in the numbers that appear in the reports because the plants use a standard set of computer-based algorithms that calculate the savings from direct labor redeployments involved in productivity improvements.

The reports of disposition are accumulated from all the plants and are reviewed at plant and VP-level meetings. A revolving report is published in the BPR database that indicates how many best practices each of the thirty-seven Vehicle Operations plants has submitted and how many each has implemented. This "public" scorecard serves as a subtle inducement to plants to both submit and adopt. Another summary scorecard tallies which plants have implemented each best practice. Having a large number of colleagues adopt a practice is a considerable source of pride for the production engineers at a source site. Steering committees in Europe and North America review these reports, and if they note that a plant under their wing is not participating adequately, a member of the steering committee calls, applying pressure to participate more fully. Thus far, the most-used practice has been replicated in thirty-five of the thirty-seven plants. The value added is, of course, in the replication. One plant may make an improvement that saves $20,000. Then if nine additional plants replicate that best practice, the saving is quickly multiplied to $200,000.

By the request of the production engineers who use it, Ford's BPR is a "push system." The engineers have made it clear that they do not want to have to search a computer database to determine if there are any new best practices that might apply to their area—they want the practices to come to them, and they want to see only best practices that apply to *their area*.

Ford's BPR system has a number of elements that work together to make it successful: (1) the database that distributes the best practices, (2) the designated production engineers in each plant who receive the items and in turn submit items, (3) plant management meetings at which decisions are made about adoption, (4) the response and tracking system that produces and distributes reports of replication activity, (5) frequent face-to-face meetings of production engineers from across Ford, (6) the plant productivity requirement that drives the continual search for new ideas to reduce costs, and (7) a small central staff of half a dozen people who maintain the system.

TEXAS INSTRUMENTS—ALERT NOTIFICATION SYSTEM

TI's interest in knowledge sharing is part of its long history of placing a high value on training and knowledge. The company was an early player in the quality effort, using the Baldrige criteria by 1990. It initiated TI-BEST in recognition that there were pockets of excellence across its different companies. TI's knowledge management effort began in 1994 after it identified a wide disparity in yields and productivity among its wafer fabrication sites. By 1995 TI had initiated a Best Practice and Lessons Learned database and had 138 worldwide facilitators or knowledge brokers who were the core of its Best Practice Sharing Program. At its height, the "Shareit" Intranet site was visited over 10,000 times a month. In 1996 TI awarded its first Not Invented Here, But I Did It Anyway (NIHBIDIA) awards. There were fifty-two nominations that resulted in two awards that were given at TI's ShareFair, the first companywide exhibition that brought almost every major organization within TI together to learn, study, and share.

After the untimely death of TI's CEO, Jerry Junkins, in 1996, a new management team brought a change of philosophy that decentralized staff functions. The Best Practice effort, as well as other central functions such as quality, metrics, and audits, was dispersed to the businesses. This meant that each business unit would determine for itself what knowledge transfer practices would be of use.

In 1997 the managers of the twenty Wafer Fab facilities around the world that made up the Semiconductor Group determined they needed four knowledge-sharing processes to improve their effectiveness: (1) a database that could archive technical reports, (2) a central site that would help people connect to other sites, (3) an electronic newsgroup where engineers could ask questions of each other, and (4) an Alert Notification System. It is the last of these, the Alert Notification System, that I focus on here as an example of Near Transfer.

The intent of the Alert Notification System is disaster avoidance. If a disaster occurs, the facility involved immediately alerts all the other facilities to the potential danger. However, for TI, the term "disaster" is not limited to safety issues but also includes, for example, an engineer becoming aware that a particular vendor is shipping bad material. Potentially, the Alert Notification System could also be used to share major breakthroughs so that others could quickly capitalize on an improvement, although, in reality, bad news is shared more frequently than good news.

To see how the Alert Notification System works we can follow Walt Jacobs, a process engineer working in TI's Dallas Wafer Fab (DFAB). He has the responsibility for the metal deposition process that places the successive layers of electrical interconnects on the silicon wafer. Walt has just received an e-mail forwarded from his own manager in DFAB. It is the kind of message that the Wafer Fab managers around the world receive every few weeks, an Alert Notification. This particular alert originated with an engineer, Antonio Rucci, who works in a Wafer Fab in Italy.

Antonio got an unexpectedly low yield on several lots of one of TI's most complex semiconductor devices, and the failure analysis revealed that this was caused by tungsten silicide instead of tungsten being deposited in the contact region. After a detailed investigation Antonio discovered that the cause of the high failure rate was that one flow controller was not controlling properly and allowed an incorrect mixture of gas. To fix the problem Antonio replaced the flow controller and changed the flow rate in the process recipe to make it less susceptible to variations. As Antonio investigated the magnitude of the problem he found that many wafer lots were affected and determined that two hundred wafers would have to be thrown away because of the incorrect mixture of gas. At $2,000 per wafer that is a big loss—big enough to qualify as a disaster. Antonio and his engineering manager reviewed the problem and determined that it qualified for an Alert Notification. He quickly wrote a short description of the problem and how it affected the products being built and sent it as an e-mail to the Wafer Fab alert e-mail address. His e-mail also noted that a longer and more explanatory report on the problem would soon be posted to TI's Wafer Fab database. When the message was sent to the alert address it was automatically replicated to all of the TI Wafer Fab managers.

In Dallas, Walt picks up the notice and recognizes it as a potential problem for the Dallas Fab. As soon as possible he calls his group together to explore how they want to fix the problem locally. The fix he and his group come up with is a little different from the one Antonio used, but without Antonio's alert, Walt would not even have known about the potential disaster. A couple of days later Walt writes out a brief report detailing the fix the DFAB used and posts it to the Alert Notification newsgroup. Over the next few weeks all of the Wafer Fabs will respond to the newsgroup about how they dealt with the issue that Antonio raised. For a few of the Wafer Fab sites the problem does not apply to their work. Some will replicate the fix that Antonio has outlined in the Alert. Others, like the Dallas Fab, may create their own solution, depending on the equipment and the processes being used.

As Walt's story shows, TI's Alert Notification System is a push system. It does not require engineers to check a database to see if any important notices have been sent. Rather the notification occurs automatically although infrequently. Similar to what happens in Ford's BPR, TI Wafer Fab managers review a scorecard at their monthly meeting that shows who did and did not respond to the alert. Since all twenty sites are "required" to respond, this review serves to prod any laggards into action before the next meeting.

The alerts that are sent out are a part of an interrelated system that is made up of (1) the "alerts" themselves, which are brief in the interest of getting them out quickly, (2) detailed explanations of the disaster and documentation that are sent to the Wafer Fab database, (3) a requirement for response, (4) the response reports that are sent to the Wafer Fab newsgroup and (5) there made available for other plants to see the "fix" that each plant has made, and (6) plant managers' monitoring the system through a scorecard.

Ernst & Young—PowerPacks

Like many large consulting companies, Ernst & Young was an early player in knowledge management. One of E&Y's most important knowledge management processes is a set of electronic databases, the KnowledgeWeb, that capture project deliverables developed by consulting teams (e.g., complex project plans, new project management techniques, presentations, and leading business solutions). These are "naturally occurring work products," meaning that they are documents that a consulting team has developed while doing work for a client. These products are collected and stored in databases that are then made accessible to other consultants, who are saved the time and expense of having to recreate the same basic documents, although all documents must be modified and tailored for different clients.

Over the past several years, Ernst & Young has been growing rapidly. In particular, its need for knowledgeable consultants in a wide variety of areas has increased dramatically. According to the firm's management, E&Y intends to continue to grow from 4,500 management consultants in 1997 to 12,000 in 2002. The serious challenge the firm faces is how to leverage the knowledge of the more senior consultants.

By the nature of their work, consultants are on the road

most of the time. Therefore to make the knowledge transfer system work, E&Y had to invest heavily in computer equipment that would allow the consultants access to the KnowledgeWeb from the field. By 1995, every E & Y consultant had been provided with a laptop computer that had a standardized "load-set" of applications, including project planning software, Microsoft Office, and Lotus Notes, to facilitate the retrieval of documents from the databases.

A simple and standardized submissions process was devised to make it easy to send work products in. The initial philosophy was to "let a thousand flowers bloom," so work products flowed in by the thousands. The documents were organized into broad categories and the databases were provided with sophisticated search engines. But in spite of those tools the databases quickly grew large and cumbersome. Users began to find that database contents were often repetitious and, more important, were of differing levels of quality.

E&Y's solution was to develop PowerPacks. These are collections of documents bundled by topic (e.g., mergers, utilities, information technology, banking, etc.) and chosen to represent the "best of the best" on a given topic (e.g., the best proposal, the best presentation, the best workplan, the best journal articles). PowerPacks are intentionally kept small enough that a user consultant can load the contents onto a laptop hard drive to work from while on the road, disconnected from the E&Y KnowledgeWeb. The management of the PowerPacks is accomplished by teams of consultants who are considered experts in each area. They are organized as Solution Teams and Revenue Teams and are given nearly complete responsibility for the content and maintenance of their own PowerPacks.

For many E&Y consultants, the KnowledgeWeb became much more effective with the advent of the PowerPacks. They were, as well, a significant step in moving responsibility away from centralized control and toward the local consultant specialists themselves.

To understand E&Y's system more fully, we can follow an E&Y consultant, Joyce Tompkins, who has just been asked by one of her clients in the petrochemical industry for a formal proposal for assisting with a new 360 degree feedback process. As is often the case, time is short. The client project director will be flying to the West Coast next week and wants to take the proposal with her to present to the board. That leaves Joyce just five days to put together a state-of-the-art proposal and presentation.

Joyce sets her cup of coffee on a table and settles into her cubicle in the Admirals Club lounge. Plugging her laptop into the telecommunications circuit, in seconds she is tied into the E&Y server through an auto-dial 1-800 number. She already knows what she is looking for—an explanation of E&Y's view on 360 degree feedback, E&Y's relative strengths in implementing 360 degree feedback, where the firm has done work before, some view of what others in the industry are doing, and the leading practices occurring in the petrochemical industry itself. She wants to tap into what knowledge Ernst & Young has learned collectively as an organization on the subject of 360 degree feedback—what would be a logical approach, how many resources would be needed, who they would be, and how much it would all cost.

Joyce pulls up the People Advantage PowerPack on-line. Available to her now is a plethora of organized information concerning all aspects of Human Resources–related processes. She first turns to the full database of well-maintained abstracts and selected articles that will help her to familiarize herself with the subject. With a user-friendly browser, she quickly finds several articles that she prints off to read later on the plane. She finds two that are particularly relevant and decides to send them to her client via the Internet.

The PowerPack lists members of the People Advantage Solution Team, but Joyce would like to find, more specifically, the specialists and veterans of 360 degree projects for E&Y worldwide. So she checks the Competency Tracking System, which contains profiles on every consultant at Ernst & Young—and the name of Bill Reese jumps out immediately. Joyce and Bill, both members of the Energy Revenue Team, had met several weeks before at one of the Energy Revenue Team Network meetings. These meetings are held every few months to get practitioners comprising a "community of practice" together to talk, to get to know each other, and to discuss lessons that have been learned—both good and bad—on particular projects that were ongoing worldwide. Bill had just finished a 360 degree feedback project working with an HR group for an oil company. A quick read through his background and his past few projects and she decides to give him a call.

After a brief telephone conversation, they agree to meet by videoconference that afternoon at 2:00, when Joyce has returned to the office. Joyce calls the office to book the videoconference so that everything will be ready when she arrives. In the meantime, Bill quickly turns to the Company Research Database and selects a detailed report on the prospective client, including a comprehensive profile of the company: its strengths and weaknesses, major investment areas, locations, subsidiaries, and key personalities and their statements in the media. He pulls together some of the most relevant presentations on 360 degree feedback, E&Y references, examples of project plans and costs, and e-mails them to Joyce.

During their videoconference that afternoon Joyce and Bill work together to develop the first draft of the proposal and select a cover and page style. Over the next two days, Joyce and Bill will finalize the document based on knowledge gained from their on-line reading and from contacts with other subject matter experts, after which Joyce will submit the entire file electronically to graphics. The entire proposal is completed in forty-eight hours and in Joyce's briefcase only three days after the client originally made the request.

E&Y spends approximately 6 percent of its revenue on knowledge management. This includes major investments in technology infrastructure that were not undertaken solely for purposes of knowledge management, but have certainly benefited that cause. In large part, this money has gone toward the building and maintenance of the technical infrastructure and supporting functions of the Center for Business Knowledge (CBK) in Cleveland, which currently has 270 employees. E&Y has over 70,000 employees of which 22,000 are client facing (consultants who meet with clients). The CBK has these client-facing consultants as its major focus.

Limiting the input of the databases to "naturally occurring work products" has the decided advantage of making submissions almost painless—consultants just attach files to the submissions form and fill out background information. Another advantage is that these work products are the type of information that, long before the KnowledgeWeb came into being, consultants had been asking each other for, because the work products represent the core knowledge of the consultants' practice. The disadvantage is that the lessons learned from working with the client are not captured, nor are they, in most cases, even derived. As one user put it, "The deliverables are useful, but they need to be combined with talking with experienced network members to get the full context."

CRITERIA RELATED TO NEAR TRANSFER

To illustrate the way the criteria can be used to determine which transfer system and related guidelines are most applicable to the type of knowledge that an organization wants to transfer, I am again going to reverse-engineer an example I have already described in some depth, Ford's BPR. As in chapter 3, I will again pose the criteria questions (left-hand column) as though Ford had determined that it should transfer knowledge (e.g., how to install bumpers more quickly) between manufacturing plants. In the right-hand column, I provide Ford's answers, which lead to the conclusion that the most effective transfer process would be Near Transfer. Ford would, therefore, in this hypothetical example, design a system based on the Near Transfer guidelines I will then outline.

1. Who the intended receiver of the knowledge is in terms of similarity of task and context

QUESTIONS	ANSWERS FOR TRANSFER BETWEEN FORD PLANTS
How similar are the task and the context of the receiving team(s) to	The tasks are very similar. At all Ford Vehicle Operations plants the molding must be wiped to ensure the seal,

| those of the source team? | the vehicle must be painted, and the bumpers must be installed. There are certainly variations in these tasks, depending on the model of vehicle and the level of automation, but the tasks are similar in all of the plants. The contexts are also similar. Walking into a plant in Saarlouis, Germany, would feel much the same as walking into the one in Wayne, Michigan. |
| Does the receiving team(s) have the absorptive capacity (experience, technical knowledge, shared language) to implement what the source team has developed? | When the team in Atlanta talks about wiping the molding for the windshield, teams in Louisville and Dearborn are fully aware of what happens when the molding is not wiped completely. The reason for wiping the molding, the sequence, and the cause and effect are a part of their shared context. Not just what happens but also why it happens is common knowledge. |

2. How routine and frequent the task is

QUESTIONS	ANSWERS FOR TRANSFER BETWEEN FORD PLANTS
How frequently does this task occur? Daily? Monthly? Yearly?	Automobile production is characterized by high-volume runs with approximately five hundred cars being produced per eight-hour shift. Each task is carried out as many as five hundred times a day.
Is the task routine or nonroutine? Are there clear steps, or is each next step variable?	The tasks are routine with almost no variation in procedure each time the task is carried out. In fact, the goal is to accomplish the tasks using standardized processes.

3. The kind of knowledge that is being transferred

QUESTIONS	ANSWERS FOR TRANSFER BETWEEN FORD PLANTS
Is the knowledge of the source team primarily tacit or explicit?	Vehicle Operations tasks involve explicit knowledge about procedures and machines. Little tacit knowledge is involved.
How many functional areas of the organization will be impacted by implementing the knowledge? One team? One division? The whole organization?	Only the receiving team is impacted by the knowledge received in the transfer. Although other parts of the factory may benefit from the increased efficiency of the team, others do not need to alter their behavior or processes to accommodate the changes that a receiving team would make.

DESIGN GUIDELINES FOR NEAR TRANSFER

KNOWLEDGE IS DISSEMINATED ELECTRONICALLY

For TI's Alert Notification System, Ford's Best Practice Replication, and E&Y's PowerPacks, the primary mechanism of transfer is electronic. Certainly, not all of Near Transfer can occur that way, but perhaps as much as 80 percent can. The remaining 20 percent, even for Near Transfer, must still be accomplished through personal interaction. However, Near Transfer and Expert Transfer (chapter 7) are the two categories in which electronic systems make the greatest contribution. As I have shown, electronic systems are of little use in Serial Transfer and will be of only minimal use in Far Transfer.

ELECTRONIC DISSEMINATION IS SUPPLEMENTED BY PERSONAL INTERACTION

The production engineers at Ford hold quarterly meetings at different plants around the world where they can examine, firsthand, the practices of sister plants. The meetings are not the core of the transfer process, yet without them the system would not work. The face-to-face meetings serve to renew the relationships among the production engineers from different factories. And as a part of that renewal the engineers reinforce, in their own minds, the fact that others are competent and knowledgeable. At the meetings production engineers talk about what they have been accomplishing and receive encouragement from others to submit the talked-about practice to the database. Best practices that have been widely replicated come up in conversation, which encourages still others to replicate them.

Likewise for the TI Wafer Fab managers. The monthly managers' meeting is an opportunity to reaffirm the usefulness of sharing knowledge about disasters. At E&Y, meetings of the solutions and revenue teams are often held quarterly. These are opportunities to share both knowledge and needs. And, as with Ford's BPR, an upturn in both submissions to the databases and hits on the databases follows such meetings.

In order for knowledge to be *put into action*, the recipients of the Near Transfer must have some level of belief that the originator of the knowledge is experienced and capable. Personal meetings provide that assurance, or what learning theorists John Seely Brown and Paul Duguid call "warrants." They note that "communities develop their own, distinct criteria for what counts as evidence and what provides 'warrants'—the endorsements for knowledge that encourage people to rely on it and hence make it actionable."[3] Most of us, from our own personal experience, would agree that this is not an unreasonable attitude. We are all reluctant to act on what others say without knowing them personally. It is through the "knowing" that we determine whether their experience is sufficient and applicable enough to trust their ideas. The need for warranting is the reason doctors and attorneys prominently display their degrees. The more consequential the situation the more necessary and specific is the requirement for warrants.

The way Ford's Best Practice Replication system began (see chapter 1), speaks to this point of warranting knowledge as well. By starting with site visits that were lengthy enough to build relationships between two groups, the production engineers established warrants for the ideas they brought back to their home sites.

USERS SPECIFY THE CONTENT AND FORMAT

It is the people who will receive the knowledge who can best identify (1) the processes that support the transfer, (2) what should be included in the transfer document, and (3) the format the document should take. When Ford began its BPR, production engineers specified what information they wanted on the submission form. They said, for example, that they wanted to see only best practices that had been proven, rather than those that were good ideas. Being proven meant they were up and running in some plant and that plant was able to put numbers to the cost involved and the savings it had accrued. After the BPR had been in place for a few months, the production engineers said it would be helpful to have pictures as well as text. And even more recently they have been saying they need video, because many of the best practices are processes that involve motion. Video, of course, requires considerably more sophisticated telecommunications equipment, which Ford is in the process of putting in place to carry video to the plants.

The design issue here is broader than someone in a central position talking with potential users about what they want in the database: it is in large part a control issue. Who is in charge of the system, those who are using it or a central group? Are units putting information in the database because they perceive a central group wants the knowledge or because the users perceive they have need of it themselves? These are not subtle distinctions. In both the Ford and the TI examples, control resides with the users.

In the E&Y example, when knowledge management was first established in 1994, it was a central group, the Center for Business Knowledge (CBK), that specified what would be in the KnowledgeWeb and how it would function. With the advent of the PowerPack, the CBK gradually began devolving content responsibility more and more to the Solution and Revenue

Teams. By 1997, the CBK had refocused its role to that of providing the expertise necessary to ensure standardized input, organization of data, and the improvement of the technology behind the KnowledgeWeb. But the content and, in particular, the selection of items for PowerPacks had devolved to the Solution Teams. Thus even in a system that was initially centralized, the only practical solution was to place control in the hands of the users themselves.

KNOWLEDGE IS PUSHED

"Pushed" in this context means that the knowledge appears automatically rather than users searching for the knowledge. In TI's case the alert appears in the managers' e-mail. At Ford it appears on the Focal Point's BPR page when he or she opens the program. In both situations the "push" is seen as a time-saving device rather than a control device. Recipients save time by not having to search for the knowledge and, more particularly, not having to read through a great deal of unrelated knowledge. Both TI and Ford have a response requirement that provides assurance that the posting was seen.

At E&Y the PowerPacks are "selected" knowledge. A team of consultants has sifted through the many submissions from teams in the field and has identified the content of the PowerPack as the "best of the best." The PowerPacks are not pushed, as is the knowledge at TI and Ford, but the PowerPack format greatly reduces the need for time-consuming searches and assures the quality of the knowledge being offered.

A LIMITED NUMBER OF ITEMS ARE PUSHED

This guideline is clearly tied to the one above. If knowledge is pushed, the number of items must be kept low and the level of quality high. At TI alerts occur about once a month. It takes a manager only a few minutes to identify to whom the alert should be forwarded and to do so. Ford Focal Points receive five to eight best practices a week, so their task of retrieval and response takes no more than a few hours a month. E&Y limits the size of each PowerPack so that it can be downloaded into a notebook computer.

THERE IS COMPLIANCE WITH CHOICE

Near Transfer systems involve a paradoxical combination of compliance and choice. At Ford there is the 5 percent task requirement, which the transferred items help meet; in fact, on average, 40 percent of the productivity improvements at Ford plants come from these best practices—and in some plants 100 percent of task is taken from the Best Practice Replication system. Another element of compliance for Ford's BPR is the requirement that Focal Points respond to every best practice that is sent to them. But the element of choice is equally present. Plants are not required to use any of the best practices that are received. They are free to say that something does not fit or would be too costly—they make use only of best practices that fit their situation.

The same is true for TI, where each Wafer Fab facility is required to respond by identifying how it will avert the potential disaster. But facilities are not required to use any specific fix and, in fact, have the choice of designing an innovative new solution.

The thinking behind the seeming paradox of compliance and choice is based on the lessons organizations have learned from years of trying, often unsuccessfully, to require teams to implement knowledge that corporate has decided everyone should use. What has become evident is that people can make use of knowledge only when their own reasoning tells them it will work. When people are forced to act against their reasoning, they may go through the motions, but they do not really absorb or apply the knowledge. No two situations are ever exactly the same, even given task and context similarity; for this reason, the judgment of whether some practice will be effective is best made by those who will implement it.

Yet left to their own initiative, many teams would not take the time to seek out new ideas, so the compliance part of the process is a necessary element. In Near Transfer, however, the compliance element is very different from offering incentives for submissions to a database or requiring statements on a performance review form. In Near Transfer, compliance is about reaching a *business goal*, and the transfer of common knowledge is a way to reach that goal.

USAGE AND BUSINESS GOALS ARE MONITORED

For Near Transfer to work it needs not only the compliance and choice elements, but also a way to monitor both usage and goal attainment. TI and Ford both track transfer with a scorecard that is reviewed by upper-level managers.

Those who are the users of the Near Transfer system also play a monitoring role. The subtle but critical pressure of the scorecard encourages the production engineers at Ford plants both to adopt transfer practices and to offer new best practices. Likewise TI engineers sending "fixes" to the newsgroup makes them available to everyone to use, or even to improve on, and it also serves to affirm the importance of the responses.

BRIEF DESCRIPTIONS ARE ADEQUATE

The reports that serve as transfer mechanisms for the knowledge in Near Transfer typically are very brief. A lengthy description is unnecessary because task and context similarity ensures that the problem is already well understood by those who are receiving the knowledge. Report formats can be standardized, making both submission and review faster, often just a matter of checking a box. E&Y brags that it takes no more than ten minutes to submit documents to the KnowledgeWeb, and Ford claims the job of Focal Point takes no more than a couple of hours a month.

THE DATABASE IS TARGETED

The knowledge that is shared through Near Transfer is targeted. TI's Alert Notification System is *only* about disasters, not about useful ideas or innovations. Likewise E&Y's PowerPacks have a limited, one topic focus.

One of the ways that many organizations get into trouble in their knowledge management efforts is by building huge multipurpose databases that contain all of the best practices from across the company. Certainly E&Y's original philosophy of "let a thousand flowers bloom" was an appealing idea. But unfortunately, even with sophisticated search engines, these systems tend to fall of their own weight. One lesson organizations have learned is to construct databases that are very targeted to a specific topic or a specific community of practice.

BUSINESS DRIVER

The goal of Near Transfer is *not* to "share knowledge" but rather to meet a specific business goal established by management. The business goal for E&Y is a reduction in the time it takes consultants to develop a proposal. With the help of PowerPacks, E&Y has reduced proposal development from an average of three weeks to three days—an enormous cost savings, since proposal development time is always a significant cost for consulting firms. The 5 percent task that Ford puts on its automotive plants drives the high level of use of the BPR system.

Management has a key role to play in identifying the business driver and in constructing a carefully thought through connection between the targeted knowledge and the business driver. However, unless those who will be receiving the knowledge also have a clear understanding of the connection, the business driver will have little impact. The connection must be real and unambiguous.

BARRIERS AND PROBLEMS

The concerns people raise about Near Transfer are often based on their own experience of having set up a little-used database or a frustrating attempt to encourage teams to use a new practice or process.

WE TRIED A BEST PRACTICE DATABASE BUT COMPANY MEMBERS DIDN'T USE IT

A database is only one of many interdependent elements that have to be in place for Near Transfer to work. Other necessary elements include (1) a well-defined business driver, (2) identified knowledge that is directly related to the business driver, (3) face-to-face meetings that serve to "warrant" the knowledge, (4) a way to publicly monitor usage and goals, and (5) designated people responsible for input and retrieval. Many companies that have set up best practice databases have put into place only one or two of the elements that are needed to make them work. Then, when the system fails, the "culture" of the organization is blamed—"people in this organization are just not willing to share their knowledge," for example.

Some organizations have first created a database with the idea that later they will add the other elements. But Near Transfer needs both to be seen as and to function as a whole. The piecemeal approach can be a self-defeating strategy.

IF IT'S NOT INVENTED HERE WE WON'T USE IT

Certain work cultures highly prize innovation and problem solving and tend to resist knowledge that they did not create themselves. But even in these cultures there is some level of knowledge sharing taking place on an informal basis. This would certainly have been true of the Vehicle Operations plants at Ford before the Best Practice Replication system was put in place. Production engineers in these plants had always had buddies they would call to ask how to shave some time off installing a bumper or to brag a little about a new piece of automated equipment they had found. Of course, not all of the production engineers were involved in this kind of informal exchange of knowledge. And a production engineer's network of buddies was probably limited to only four or five people in other plants. Nevertheless, the exchange of knowledge did go on, as it does in all organizations. What Ford was able to do was to build on the knowledge exchange that was already happening, turning a naturally occurring phenomenon into something that is more systematic, widespread, and accessible.

If an organization is faced with a culture that is steeped in independent problem solving, an excellent place to begin is to find out *who* is already sharing information, *what* information they are already sharing, and *why* those who are asking for the knowledge need it. Armed with this knowledge it is possible to construct a Near Transfer system that fits the culture. Those who are already sharing knowledge know the most about how to expand the informal system to bring in peers who can use the knowledge. Building on what already exists is far more effective than trying to change the culture by bringing in something new.

People Don't Have Time to Share

A sure way to kill any interest in transferring knowledge is to tell those who have done really innovative work that they now have to spend half a day writing it up for others. Near Transfer works because the similarity between source and receiving teams means lengthy reports are not necessary. If it is not possible to transfer the knowledge with brevity, then it is probably not explicit knowledge that is being transferred; it may be tacit or a complex combination of tacit and explicit knowledge— and databases don't work for that kind of knowledge. In such a case, the organization will have to construct a system based on the guidelines for Strategic Transfer or Far Transfer that I will outline in later chapters. It is making the match between type of knowledge and transfer system that is critical.

Summary

Near Transfer is about sharing explicit knowledge between teams that do very similar work in very similar contexts. Computer technology provides a very effective way to disseminate explicit common knowledge, although it cannot do the job alone. Each of the effective systems described here has combined technology with face-to-face meetings that serve to "warrant" the knowledge.

Near Transfer is often the category where organizations choose to initiate their knowledge-sharing activities, perhaps because "best practice" is a familiar concept and the need to share best practice is readily acknowledged in most organizations. It is also the category where results are most easily tracked, so it allows an organization to tout the cost savings that have been made. Such strong evidence that sharing explicit knowledge works can gain acceptance for other kinds of knowledge sharing that may not be so quantifiable.

But there is also a danger in starting with Near Transfer. Because of the very visible technology element of Near Transfer, the temptation is to simply turn the "project" over to the technology group, to let it build the system. That is a very powerful temptation, especially when everyone expects that to be the solution and the technology group is more than willing to take on the task. But the technology group can't put into place all of the interwoven elements that are necessary to make Near Transfer work. One of those critical elements is finding a way to combine compliance with choice. That combination has to be carefully and skillfully constructed by those who have the authority to require compliance. But when compliance and choice are combined effectively, the result eliminates many of the concerns that are thought of as culture-based, for example, "not invented here." The successful combination eliminates, as well, the need for contrived incentives or elaborate campaigns to encourage use.

Table 4–1 shows the design guidelines for Near Transfer. Of importance is the difference in transfer criteria between Near Transfer and Serial Transfer. While Near Transfer involves routine knowledge, Serial Transfer is focused on nonroutine knowledge. Serial Transfer involves both tacit and explicit knowledge, while Near Transfer focuses only on explicit knowledge. These differences lead to very different guidelines for how transfer happens.

TABLE 4-1

DESIGN GUIDELINES FOR NEAR TRANSFER

Definition	Explicit knowledge a team has gained from doing a frequent and repeated task is reused by other teams doing very similar work.
Similarity of task and context	The receiving team does a task similar to that of the source team and in a similar context.
Nature of the task	Frequent and routine
Type of knowledge	Explicit
Design guidelines	Knowledge is disseminated electronically
	Electronic dissemination is supplemented by personal interaction
	Users specify the content and format
	Knowledge is pushed
	A limited number of items are pushed
	There is compliance with choice
	Usage and business goals are monitored
	Brief descriptions are adequate
	The database is targeted
Example	A team in an Atlanta auto plant figures out how to install brakes in ten seconds. A team in Chicago uses that knowledge to reduce its time by fifteen seconds.

In the next chapter we will look at the third type of transfer, Far Transfer, and will consider some examples and then the guidelines that make this kind of transfer effective.

CHAPTER 5

FAR
TRANSFER

*Helen is a team leader for British Petroleum's Barden Explora-
tion site. She has four people reporting to her: two geophysicists,
a geologist, and a petroleum engineer. The team has spent several
months collecting and analyzing a great deal of data about the
possible well site off the coast of Norway known as Barden.
The team is at a point where it needs to make a decision on
how to proceed. Should BP commit to a rig? Should it make
firm commitments to its partners in the exploration license?
These are important decisions because of the money involved;
for example, a rig, can cost up to $200 a minute!*

 *Helen's team has decided it would be useful for her to call
upon the knowledge that other people in BP have learned about
this type of prospect, that is, to call for a Peer Assist. That
means identifying people from other parts of the world who
have experience with the kind of issues facing the Barden team.
Helen identifies about fifteen possible candidates, people she has*

worked with before or knows about through the grapevine. She makes the calls. She finds some are too busy on other projects, but she ends up with seven people from her original list that she thinks can be very helpful: three from the Norway office, one from Scotland, one from South Africa, and two from London. They have agreed to meet on a Wednesday, one month from now, in Stavanger, Norway, to spend the day.

On the meeting day, Helen starts by defining what her team wants from the Peer Assist. She lays out the objectives for the meeting. The Peer Assist members have received a packet of material to read through in advance. The walls of the conference room where Helen's team and the Peer Assisters are meeting are covered with pictures of the ocean bed, seismic lines, and charts. More documents are spread several layers deep on the tables around the room. As Helen finishes her introduction, the Peer Assist group asks some clarification questions about the objectives, then Helen introduces Knut, who begins to talk through the data and his interpretation of it. Before long everyone is up looking more closely at the wall displays. A lively discussion ensues about the implications of various factors.

After a coffee break, Martin, another member of Helen's team, begins to show the data for seismic velocity. Again within minutes the whole group is back on its feet examining the charts more closely. The discussion flows back and forth with the Peer Assist members asking each other technical questions about the data and often challenging each other's responses.

After the lunch break, Helen says that they have finished presenting the data they planned. The Peer Assist group returns to questions about the original objectives for clarification in light of what they have just heard. One of the Peer Assisters notes: "I'm uncomfortable with the discussion because there are some strategic decisions to be made before we can give our opinion on whether to drill the well." The group decides it needs to develop criteria for drilling the Barden well. Collaboratively the two groups develop these criteria, gaining additional insight as they talk through each point.

About three o'clock Helen says she would like to excuse herself and her team to give the assist team a chance to talk through the response it wants to make. Once the Barden team leaves the room, the Peer Assist group designates one member to keep track of its ideas on the flip charts and considers who should make the report when the team returns. As the group gets down to work on its recommendations there is an animated exchange. For nearly every assertion that is made, someone wants to know why that is needed or why it should be given preference over other points. The member from Scotland suggests a new technique his team has just developed west of the Shetlands that could provide useful additional data on a prospect like Barden. He offers to send the specifications for that process and to spend some time helping the Barden team go through it the first time. The discussion is technical but it is very open and lively. It is obvious that the members are interested in this situation and want to be of help.

About five o'clock the Barden team returns to hear the ideas of the assist team. The spokesperson thanks the Barden team for giving them a chance to work on such an interesting problem and notes they have all learned from the exchange. The verbal report is given with the promise of a more formal written report later. As the report proceeds the Barden team asks a few clarification questions, but mostly the members listen to the thoughtful response the Peer Assisters are providing. When the report is finished, Helen says that the report is very clear and notes that it has given her team a great deal to think about as it moves toward the decisions it must make. She acknowledges that the Barden team was nervous about whether it was too early in its investigation to call for a Peer Assist, but she is now convinced that the timing was right. The team can take the recommendations into account before it is fully committed to a course of action. The day ends with dinner at a local restaurant. The dinner is relaxed and people have time to talk through how the Peer Assist went. The dinner is a way for the Barden team to express its gratitude to those who came to lend their knowledge.

Far Transfer is applicable when a team has learned something from its experience that the organization would like to make available to other teams that are doing similar work. If I stopped there, the description would sound no different than Near Transfer. There are, however, two important additional criteria, and the first relates to the nature of the task. The task that is the subject of Far Transfer is *nonroutine* whereas the task in Near Transfer is routine. The Peer Assist story illustrates a nonroutine task—the task of exploration. The exploration of a site could not be done the same way each time it is undertaken because the results of an initial study of the site could send geologists down any one of many paths, and each subsequent path would again raise many possible new leads to follow. Experience in working at other sites helps petroleum engineers and geophysicists make better interpretations of the data they review in making decisions at each juncture, but they cannot predict a path.

The second significant difference between Near Transfer and Far Transfer is that Far Transfer is applicable when the knowledge that the source team has gained is largely tacit rather than explicit. The exploration example illustrates the way that the tacit knowledge of the assisters is drawn from them by the situation the Barden team is facing.

Like the label "Near," the term "Far" is borrowed from learning theorists. The term "Far" indicates that the receiving team is likely to be very different from those who are the source of the knowledge. It may be in a different geographic location, with a different culture, using a different technology, and with a different set of competitors. When the transfer is "Far," the knowledge from the source team has to be translated or considerably modified for it to be applicable to the receiving team. It is not possible simply to take what has been learned in one setting and reuse it in another because the setting itself is too different.

Examples of Far Transfer

I provide three examples of Far Transfer: BP's Peer Assist, which I have described in the opening story; Chevron's Capital Project Management; and Lockheed Martin's LM21 Best Practice.

BRITISH PETROLEUM—PEER ASSIST

Peer Assist was initiated at British Petroleum by a study team of mid-level managers who, late in 1994, were charged with establishing a way business units could provide greater support and assurance for each other within the framework of the federation model recently adopted by BP. In moving to a federation model business units had greater autonomy and the corporate group much less direct quality control on the work of the business units. Peer Assist was conceived as a way that one business unit could call upon another business unit for help, rather than assistance coming from the corporate level.

As a member of the study team, Andrew Mackenzie initially coordinated the Peer Assists. Business units that wanted to hold a Peer Assist called Mackenzie to help identify people who might be of assistance. He also worked with the project leader to establish the objectives of the assist and to collect the lessons learned that resulted. The Peer Assist process quickly gained credibility within British Petroleum, and after the first twenty to thirty Peer Assists had been conducted with Mackenzie's help, they simply began to happen spontaneously. Team leaders who were thinking about holding a Peer Assist were confident enough about the process, which after all was quite simple, that they no longer felt a need to call the study team for assistance.

In the ensuing years hundreds, if not thousands, of Peer Assists have been held across all parts of BP. Peer Assists spread across BP because people quickly found that they helped them get their work done more effectively. There is a strong conviction among BP employees that Peer Assist gives BP an edge over competitors. People who are asked to do the assisting view it as a kind of honor or recognition. They want to see what is happening in other parts of the company because doing so helps them advance in the company. However, being on a Peer Assist is still viewed as extra—on top of your regular job. And for this reason groups feel pressure to make the Peer Assist as short as they can, most being from one to three days in length.

Peer Assist has become the "before" piece of British Petroleum's three-part knowledge management process. BP has published a simple one-page brochure that explains what Peer Assist is and provides ten golden rules for new users of the process. However, the golden rules are broad, such as, "Be clear in articulating the business problem or challenge you are asking the group to help with, and the objective of the assist." It is up to the team asking for the assist to design the experience in the way that it deems most useful. Some Peer Assists have brought in an intact team to help. That happened with one of the exploration teams in the North Sea, which brought in a team from the Gulf of Mexico, one of the few other places that had experience drilling in such deep water. Other teams asking for an assist choose individuals from different business units to comprise the assisting team—the story at the beginning of this chapter was that kind of situation. Some Peer Assists are held early in the work of a team, and some at a later time. The golden rule in the brochure about when to hold a Peer Assist states, "A Peer Assist is appropriate when the cost of gathering the help leverages significant potential business benefits, when a business unit is facing a challenge that others may be able to offer experience and insight to. It is appropriate when the diversity of views external to the Business Unit can broaden the range of options considered."

There was considerable discussion early in the evolution of the Peer Assist process about who should pay for the cost of the travel. Although still not standard across all units, it is generally agreed that cross charging creates too much paperwork. The business unit that is sending an assister pays, recognizing that it will receive a corresponding benefit when it has need of an assist. Overall the process is reciprocal enough that who pays appears not to be a critical issue.

CHEVRON—CAPITAL PROJECT MANAGEMENT

Capital Project Management is a critical process for Chevron because the company spends over $5 billion a year on capital projects. At any one time there may be as many as 220 capital projects within the company. Upon the completion of the benchmark of sixty companies in 1991, Chevron realized that it was at the bottom in terms of cycle time and amount of rework done on capital projects. In response Chevron developed a process for capital project management, Chevron Project Development & Execution Process (CPDEP), that it considers to be an industrywide best practice. CPDEP is resourced by the Project Resources Group, which is composed of a core group of fifteen project consultants and a larger group of one hundred project managers experienced with the CPDEP tools. The core team consists of professionals who have developed special competence with the CPDEP tools, for example, benchmarking or industry comparable data. The mission of the core team, whose members are selected for their leadership and consensus-building skills, is to bring this expertise to major capital projects and to collect and spread the knowledge learned from other projects. These professionals see themselves as facilitating the movement of the organization's knowledge across its boundaries.

The Project Resources Group believes that the optimum way to move knowledge is to move people, so its job involves physically moving around Chevron to spread the lessons that have been learned. The group also sponsors two forums each year designed as knowledge exchanges between project managers. Recently, the Project Resources Group was reorganized to become a profit center, selling its services and knowledge to project managers within Chevron.

To see how the Project Resources Group works we can follow Henry Gonzales, who has been a project manager for Chevron for over six years and during that time has managed three very critical and successful projects. At least he thought of them as successful until last October, when he attended a Project Management Forum put on by Project Resources. At the time he attended the meeting, Henry's third project was nearing completion. But to his dismay while he was there he discovered that there were two other Chevron project teams, in other parts of the country, that had engaged in projects very similar to his: one that had completed six months earlier, and one that had completed three months earlier. One of them had developed a process that, had he known about it, could have saved him three months. Henry was really kicking himself about that one. The other project appeared to have made several of the same mistakes Henry's team had made, only it had made them three months earlier. So if Henry had been able to learn from that project's mistakes, it might have saved his project up to $80,000. "If he had known" seemed to be the operative term.

Now Henry is ready to begin his fourth project, building a reformulated gasoline facility (a process plant that will convert certain types of gasoline blending components into cleaner-burning fuels). And Henry is committed to learning from the knowledge that is within Chevron, and what is more, he has a way to access that knowledge. The first thing he does is to put a call in to the Project Resources Group to contract with Jerry, one of the consultants that he got acquainted with at the forum. Henry knows he will have to pay for these services, but with a project that is estimated to cost right at $400 million, it will be worth it to have Jerry link him up with past and current projects that he can learn from. Henry saw the evidence with his own eyes when he was at the forum. Using the tools, contacts, and knowledge of the Project Resources Group could potentially save him up to 20 percent on the project and save him time as well.

Henry and Jerry will start by getting together for about a week to plan the whole development of the project. Together they will assess the skills of the project team as it is currently resourced, identify needed people, and Jerry will develop a series of workshops tailored to the specific needs of Henry's team. Another source that Henry has at his fingertips is a database that will let him know what current projects he can look to for state-of-the-art practice in several areas he wants to focus on. Safety is one that he is interested in, and since this will be a joint venture with BP, he will want to find out who has developed the best practices with joint ventures. He will follow up with the leads he finds in the database, making telephone calls and site visits. He will also look to Jerry to point him in the direction of current projects he or his team members should visit.

Over the two years it will take to complete the project, Jerry will spend nearly two months working with Henry. During this time he will contribute ideas he has gained from similar projects. And he will bring state-of-the-art project management tools such as front-end loading, internal and external benchmarking, industry comparable data, and an independent peer review process. Jerry will be on call for Henry in a mentoring and coaching relationship during all phases of the project. Finally, Jerry will assist with the formal review process that all projects are required to make at the time of appropriation of the funds. Jerry's help in the final phase will assist Henry in bringing the project to a successful close, but equally important, it will help Jerry prepare for his larger task of sharing the lessons learned in this project with other projects he will work on in the future.

Jerry sees himself as a kind of living database that carries the knowledge of the organization from site to site. One way of doing that will be to connect Henry and some of his key project team members with new teams that are starting and that could benefit from what Henry has learned on this project. However, what Henry is looking forward to with great anticipation is being in the next Project Management Forum and having the opportunity to tell others what he and his team learned through doing the project. He can almost hear some poor project manager saying, "If only I had known."

Although there is a database in place for CPDEP, as there was for Ford (see chapter 4), the database is not the central element of this system. What makes this system work are the internal consultants who are able to spend enough time with a project team to really understand the specifics of the project they are undertaking and through this in-depth understanding are able to call on their own tacit knowledge for ideas. Equally important, the in-depth knowledge allows them to suggest other teams and sites for team members to visit so that they can gain additional tacit knowledge from those teams.

LOCKHEED MARTIN—LM21 BEST PRACTICES

The defense industry has been faced with a continually shrinking Defense budget which has brought about a need for increased productivity and has fostered industrywide mergers and acquisitions. Lockheed Martin, a major player in the industry restructuring, is currently made up of more than thirty operating companies, or business units, originating from seventeen different heritage corporations, including Lockheed, Martin Marietta, Xerox, GE Aerospace, Loral, IBM, and General Dynamics. The products and services covered by this span of companies range from jet fighters to complex electronics, and from high technology manufacturing to information systems.

The LM21 Best Practices approach was designed to share knowledge across all Lockheed Martin operating companies in response to the ongoing need for cost reduction and productivity improvement. LM21 is a follow-on to the restructuring effort that began in 1995 to eliminate duplicate or redundant facilities, capabilities, structures, and support that were the result of the mergers. By early 1999 that consolidation effort had yielded $2.6 billion in annual savings. The goal Lockheed Martin established for LM21 was to at least match what had been achieved through the restructuring—that is, to achieve an additional $2.6 billion by 2002 through the sharing of knowledge. LM21 Best Practices began with Engineering but soon extended to cover all major cost functions, including program management, operations, employee development, indirect cost, and procurement.

To initiate this effort, Lockheed Martin conducted an extensive internal benchmarking effort across forty-seven of its internal sites and thirty-two external companies. It benchmarked some seventy practices within the six major cost functions. What it learned was that none of the Lockheed Martin operating companies was best at everything on the list and, equally important, nearly every company was best at something! This was a revealing study to many of the internal business units that had considered themselves "best in class" on nearly every process they used. And it confirmed that the transfer of these practices was needed because, "The level of capability that existed in the Corporation was far beyond the capability of any one company."[1]

The benchmark study, which was the largest of its kind ever conducted, encouraged many of the companies to begin efforts to transfer knowledge through their informal networks. And although the informal effort resulted in some cost savings, it became clear that Lockheed Martin was not going to achieve its goal without a more structured approach.

LM21 Best Practices provided that structured approach. Lockheed Martin put together over thirty "transfer teams," each made up of representatives from eight different operating companies. For example, the "design to value" transfer team has representatives from two "source" companies, both of which made high benchmark scores on "design to value." The other six members represent "receiving" sites, units that chose to be a part of the "design to value" transfer team because that practice was one in which they saw a need for improvement at their own site. Each transfer team has an executive-level team leader who received special training in the transfer activities. The team members are senior Subject Matter Experts (SMEs) and senior-level decision makers or influencers from their respective units.

Individual operating companies typically are receivers for several best practice areas and serve as sources for one or two. In mid-1999, there was an average of seven inbound practices across the thirty-two participating companies. Equally impressive, twenty-one different companies served as the source of at least one best practice. Each transfer team works together over a period of several months to help members develop business cases and implementation plans for each of the receiving sites. This design builds reciprocity in on several levels: the source team members provide knowledge and are themselves learning from the receiving team members; the source teams learn from each other, since two units serve in the source role on each team; and the receiving teams can become source teams for other practices.

Each company has been assigned a portion of the targeted $2.6 billion goal, which is tracked on a Lockheed Martin–wide report card. The quarterly report card provides two scores, one for financial performance and another for participation. The report card also functions as an early warning system that allows management to step in and assist where appropriate.[2] Lockheed is averaging $2 to $10 million in savings for each receiving company for each transfer.

The LM21 Best Practices program at Lockheed Martin is a demonstration of a successful change management effort. Such change programs are hard to implement, and it is even harder to demonstrate financial results. It is likely that this succeeded at Lockheed Martin due to the extensive commitment of management at all levels of the corporation to leverage the rich diversity of the seventeen heritage corporations, as well as the development and implementation of the structured transfer process.

The next section spells out what an organization needs to put into place in order to have an effective system for Far Transfer. First I apply the three criteria for selection of a transfer process to the Peer Assist example. Then I outline the design principles based on these criteria.

CRITERIA RELATED TO FAR TRANSFER

To illustrate the criteria related to Far Transfer, I return to the example of British Petroleum's Peer Assist program. The answers to the questions posed in the left hand column make clear how different the knowledge that the exploration team has to deal with is from the explicit, routine knowledge of Near Transfer.

1. Who the intended receiver of the knowledge is in terms of similarity of task and context

QUESTIONS	ANSWERS FOR TRANSFER BETWEEN BP EXPLORATION TEAMS
How similar are the task and the context of the receiving team(s) to those of the source team?	Each team is dealing with the task of exploration, but for each team exploration takes place in a different context with differing political, legal, technological, and environmental considerations.
Does the receiving team(s) have the absorptive capacity (experience, technical knowledge, shared language) to implement what the source team has developed?	The absorptive capacity of exploration teams may vary by the experience level of the team members. Each team is newly constructed and may represent a wide range of knowledge and skills. However, the ability of teams to choose their own assisters helps to address that issue.

2. How routine and frequent the task is

QUESTIONS	ANSWERS FOR TRANSFER BETWEEN BP EXPLORATION TEAMS
How frequently does this task occur? Daily? Monthly? Yearly?	An exploration project can take up to two years to complete. Across the company there may be thirty-some teams in various stages of an exploration project.
Is the task routine or nonroutine? Are there clear steps, or is each next step variable?	The tasks are nonroutine. Exploration is never done the same way twice. Every site is different, presenting its own unique characteristics.

3. The kind of knowledge that is being transferred

QUESTIONS	ANSWERS FOR TRANSFER BETWEEN BP EXPLORATION TEAMS
Is the knowledge of the source team primarily tacit or explicit?	The knowledge is primarily tacit. It is in the heads of the team members and moreover is tied to a specific site they have been studying. Rather than the recipient of the knowledge specifying what information is required, it is the situation itself that triggers, in the minds of the assisters, what relevant ideas to offer.
How many functional areas of the organization will be impacted by implementing the knowledge? One team? One division? The whole organization?	Only the receiving team is impacted by the knowledge received in the transfer. Although the result of its interpretation impacts others, the knowledge transferred to it from other teams impacts only the receivers' thinking and actions.

DESIGN GUIDELINES FOR FAR TRANSFER

The remarkable thing about the three examples I have provided for Far Transfer is how different they are from each other. Earlier, when I described Serial Transfer and Near Transfer, the examples differed from company to company, but were recognizable as having a similar format. However, with Far Transfer we see that the structure or format of BP's Peer Assist is very unlike that of Chevron's Project Resources Group, which is very unlike that of Lockheed Martin's LM21 Best Practice. Thus the reader may be thinking, "Why are such different transfer processes all in the same category?" Although the differences are striking, these examples contain similarities that are based on the criteria for the transfer of tacit and nonroutine knowledge between teams doing similar tasks. So the good news is that there is not just one way to make this kind of transfer happen. The bad news is that the way to make this kind of transfer is largely situation dependent and therefore less easy to replicate. There are, however, guidelines to the design of such a system, which I provide here.

Exchange Is Reciprocal

The exchanges that occur in Far Transfer are reciprocal rather than one-way. Particularly with LM21 and Peer Assist, reciprocity is built into the design. When people agree to go on a Peer Assist, they know they will leave with more knowledge than they came with. They learn from the team that has asked for the assist, from their colleagues who have also come along, and from the situation itself. The way LM21 is designed facilitates reciprocity by always having two source teams on a transfer team and by making sure every unit functions in both source and receiving roles. The same is true for Chevron's project leaders, who learn from the site visits to other projects and also host teams coming to their sites. It is one thing to hope that a reciprocal exchange will take place, and another thing to design reciprocity into the transfer process itself.

Source Team Knowledge Is Translated

Far Transfer demands that what has been learned be translated into a different form for the use of the receiving team.

Because the contexts of the teams are so different, the knowledge is not usable until it has been customized. Either the receiving team itself must make the translation, or the source team must make the translation on the basis of the situation the receiving team is in.

LM21 is an example of each receiving team making the translation for itself. The source teams are there to provide ideas, but each receiving team must take those ideas and recreate them in a form that is usable for its own unit. It is obvious that "design for value" in Air Traffic Control is going to be considerably different from "design for value" in Integrated Business Solutions. So LM21 requires that each receiving unit create its own implementation plan and business plan tailored to its own situation. The other members of the transfer team are expected to help, but only those members and their back home colleagues can fully make the translation.

Peer Assist is an example of the source team making the translation. It does so by going to the site and using the specifics of the site situation to drive what knowledge is transferred.

In either configuration, the source team does not expect to say, "Here is what we did; you should do it the same way." Rather the issue is "How can what we did be translated into something that is usable in your situation?" In any transfer situation some amount of translation is always needed. In Near Transfer it is minor, in Far Transfer it is extensive.

PEOPLE CARRY THE TACIT KNOWLEDGE ACROSS THE ORGANIZATION

Living databases, that is people, have an advantage over electronic databases in that people have the ability to understand a specific situation and then tailor their response to that situation. The elements of a new situation can trigger people's tacit memory so that they can call up ideas and solutions from other situations they have experienced that are applicable to this situation. They can eliminate those that are too simplistic or in other ways are not a good fit. In the Peer Assist example, the knowledge of the peers who assisted the Barden team was largely tacit, in that it was probably not available to them until the situation itself drew it out. Stimulated by a situation, sources may be able to put together two ideas from their tacit knowledge that they have never put together before, to arrive at a totally new way to think about the situation. It is the tacit knowledge embedded in the minds of human beings that makes Far Transfer work.

Organizations have devised many ways to use people to transfer tacit knowledge in addition to the ones I have offered as examples above. At Chaparral Steel a team that develops a new process is subsequently and deliberately dispersed among the rest of the crews to diffuse the knowledge. This is not a one-time event but a policy that enhances knowledge transfer. Thomas Davenport and Laurence Prusak, authors of books on knowledge management, tell about Dai-Ichi Pharmaceuticals in Japan, where researchers are expected to spend twenty minutes each day in "talk rooms."[3] Here they discuss their current work with whoever has come in for tea. Davenport and Prusak comment, "It is a kind of Brownian motion theory of knowledge exchange, its very randomness encouraging the discovery of new ideas that a more specifically directed discussion would miss." The World Bank holds frequent Knowledge Fairs and Dow Chemical holds Technology Fairs, both designed to bring people together to exchange knowledge.

Process Is Given a Recognizable Name

In any company it is possible for a project leader to make a site visit to another project or to call in colleagues to help with a tricky issue. What is different about the examples that I have given here is that the processes have names: Project Management Resources and Peer Assist. Naming a transfer process gives organizational members a way to reference it. It moves a request for knowledge beyond that of an individual asking for help, to participating in a sanctioned activity of the organization. So the first, and perhaps most important, reason for naming a knowledge transfer process is that it legitimates the activity.

As a legitimate/named activity, the process removes a request for knowledge from the category of favors and places it in the realm of legitimate business processes that produce faster and more effective results. Without this sanction, as one engineer told me, "There are only so many times you can ask before you feel like you are being a pest or a bother, not that anyone says so, of course. But when it's all one way it gets awkward."

I also think that the label that is used makes a significant difference. Peer Assist plays better than Help Team. LM21 sounds better than Getting up to Speed. Names that have a business ring to them have less of an "asking for help" connotation. A clever exception was TI's NIHBIDIA award, which poked fun at its own organizational norms (see chapter 4).

BUSINESS DRIVER

The business driver for Far Transfer is identified at the corporate level. BP's need was to provide business units the assistance they needed to make very expensive and critical decisions—a kind of assurance. For Chevron, the goal was to reduce the costs of capital projects. In a three-year period transferring knowledge saved the company $816 million. For Lockheed Martin, the business driver is to increase productivity in the face of reduced defense spending. The goal is $2.6 billion by 2002. All of these examples had high-level and visible support.

BARRIERS AND PROBLEMS

The task of transferring tacit knowledge seems particularly problematic, perhaps because the knowledge itself seems so intangible and half-formed.

WE DON'T KNOW HOW TO GET KNOWLEDGE OUT OF PEOPLE'S HEADS

Tacit knowledge cannot be transferred by getting it out of people's heads and onto paper. Tacit knowledge can be transferred by moving the people who have the knowledge around.

It might be technically possible to get everything a person knew about some important topic down on paper, but even if that occurred, the result would not be very usable. The reason is that tacit knowledge is not only the facts but the relationships among the facts—that is, how people might combine certain facts to deal with a specific situation. People with extensive tacit knowledge about a subject may encounter a situation that they have never seen before and be able to figure out how to deal with it because it bears a slight resemblance to some other situation or because they suddenly see how two unrelated bits of knowledge can come together in this situation. It might be possible to get down on paper the tacit knowledge someone used in a past situation, but not what that person would use in any and all new situations. Calling on tacit knowledge is not just a memory task, it is as often an act of creation or invention.

Moving people physically, whether sending them off on site visits or calling Peer Assists, is what companies are trying to avoid by turning to technology. So it sounds counterintuitive to say, "Just put the knowledge on a plane and send it to some team that needs it." But not all knowledge needs to be moved by moving people; it is specifically tacit knowledge that carries this requirement. Explicit knowledge can be sent electronically, as I described in the chapter on Near Transfer. And in the next chapter I will talk about another way to move knowledge without moving people. Being selective about what knowledge is moved through people and what knowledge is moved electronically is the key.

Besides the three different ways to move tacit knowledge described in this chapter, companies use still other ways. Some organizations have begun to designate certain knowledgeable people as "shared resources," declaring that 10 percent (or 15 percent or 20 percent) of their time is to be spent sharing their knowledge companywide, leaving the other 90 percent for a specific project. One example of this strategy is E&Y, which has set up a number of industry-related networks that represent key areas of consulting practice (e.g., automotive, mergers, energy, manufacturing, health care). Assigned to each network are a few senior consultants who hold much of the tacit knowledge about that area. E&Y designates a limited number of the specialist consultants as "hard tagged"; that is, they are assigned to be dedicated learners and teachers for a period of time, visiting key projects, assisting with the development of key service offerings, delivering presentations at network meetings, and coaching other projects on leading project practices and techniques prior to startup. This is a key investment for E&Y to make in an industry that is run on billable hours—a testament to its determination to leverage tacit knowledge as well as the explicit knowledge it places in its large KnowledgeWeb.

OUR PEOPLE WON'T ASK FOR HELP

In any organization—even the most macho—there are people who call on each other for help: they pick up the phone or drop by a friend's office. In any organization there are also those to whom others come for help, people others recognize as particularly knowledgeable or helpful. That is often a good place to start—with those who are interested or are already involved, even if on a small scale.

Not everybody in an organization has to participate in order to make Far Transfer work. Even a small percentage of people sharing knowledge, 10 percent or 15 percent, can build a knowledge-sharing culture.[4] But that small percentage can build the culture only if they have a way to reference it; that is, what they are doing must have a name (such as Peer Assist). If the knowledge transfer is kept as an unnamed informal action, then little will change in the organization. If the formal transfer process starts with those who are interested and is then given a name, that makes it easier for others to participate when the need arises.

SUMMARY

Far Transfer is applicable when a team has gained tacit knowledge from its experience that the organization would like to make available to other teams that are doing similar work.

TABLE 5-1

Design Guidelines for Far Transfer

Definition	Tacit knowledge a team has gained from doing a nonroutine task is made available to other teams doing similar work in another part of the organization.
Similarity of task and context	The receiving team does a task similar to that of the source team but in a different context.
Nature of the task	Frequent and nonroutine
Type of knowledge	Tacit
Design guidelines	Exchange is reciprocal
	Source team knowledge is translated
	People carry the knowledge across the organization
	Process is given a recognizable name
Example	Peers travel to assist a team dealing with a unique oil exploration site. The collaboration provides new approaches.

Even when Far Transfer is successful, as it is in the examples I have used to illustrate it here, the process still feels insubstantial. There is something much more tangible about building a database—you can count items, track hits, even demo it. With Far Transfer a great deal of knowledge transfer may be happening, but it is harder to point to.

Despite this drawback Far Transfer is critical to organizations. Most of the knowledge that makes an organization competitive is its tacit, not its explicit, knowledge. That is why companies steal each other's employees and provide stock options to keep the ones it has. So to write off tacit knowledge as "difficult to transfer" is to ignore a company's most valuable knowledge asset.

When people say tacit knowledge is "difficult to transfer,"

they mean it is difficult to transfer by writing it down. Far Transfer requires a shift in thinking about how to make knowledge transfer happen. It works by moving the people who have the knowledge—by putting people together.

Table 5–1 shows the design guidelines for Far Transfer. In the next chapter we will again see that when tacit knowledge is an important element, bringing people together will be a factor in the design guidelines.

CHAPTER 6

STRATEGIC TRANSFER

Steve was given the responsibility to reduce the cost of British Petroleum's Venezuela operation from $70 million to $40 million—almost by half—and he was given just seven weeks to get the job done. In this brief period his change team of eight would have to:

- *create the design for the new organization,*

- *develop a plan for staff selection,*

- *determine how it would meet the financial goals,*

- *design the human resources packages that would be offered, and*

- *come up with a communication and implementation plan for each element.*

The team realized that it would not have time to reinvent the wheel; it would have to learn what it could from units that had already experienced restructuring.

Colombia was an obvious choice of a unit to learn from since it had been through a restructuring several months earlier. So those team members who knew someone in the Colombia Asset began to call to get any advice their contacts could offer. Sometimes the calls resulted in useful conversations, but sometimes the person on the other end of the line was too busy to talk or hadn't been involved enough in the specifics to help. However, before Steve's team was very far into its work, one of the chance phone calls reached someone who suggested they check out the Knowledge Asset on restructuring on BP's Intranet, because that was where the Columbia team had organized the lessons it had learned from its own restructuring process. That suggestion proved to be a turning point for the Venezuela change team.

The Venezuela change team began to try out different parts of the Restructuring Knowledge Asset. Initially the overview section was helpful because it showed where there were similarities and differences between the two change projects. The overview of the Colombia project also alerted the Venezuela team that it had not put enough emphasis on communication. Particularly helpful was reading the Q & A exchange that went on between the organizational members and the Colombia change team. This was not a summary, but the actual questions asked and the answers given by the change team. This level of detail allowed the Venezuela team to get a real feel for the kinds of concerns and questions the people in Colombia had experienced. On the basis of these insights the Venezuela change team modified its developing plans, including the addition of more communication opportunities than it had started with.

Once the Venezuela team began to use the Restructuring Knowledge Asset, its calls to Colombia were no longer random or guided by chance associations. Drawing on the many direct quotes from people who had been personally involved in Colombia, the Venezuela team was able to determine who had knowledge about specific issues it was dealing with and then a team member could call the Colombia person to get the further details he or she needed. Because the Knowledge Asset often provided differing opinions on a subject, the team found it a much richer source of information than a more typical end-of-project report that provides only the agreed-upon final solution.

The Venezuela team found that the Knowledge Asset offered two types of knowledge assistance. First, it provided the "big picture" that allowed the Venezuela team to gain an overall understanding of the Colombia project, the elements involved, and the major lessons the Colombian team had learned. This type of knowledge afforded the team a level of assurance that it was on the right track. The team made considerable use of this knowledge during the front end of the project. Then came a period of time when the Venezuela change team worked pretty much on its own without a lot of interaction with either the Knowledge Asset or the Colombia team members. But team members found themselves going back to the Knowledge Asset near the end of their planning. As they began to work on the details they were able to make use of the examples and specifics. In the Knowledge Asset they found time charts that outlined when those who were to be laid off were notified and when their supervisors were informed. They found HR plans that were differentiated for (1) the expatriate staff who would be returning to their home countries, (2) local people who might have been employed for a couple of years, and (3) staff who would be going to other countries. Of course, it was not possible for the Venezuela team to just cross out Colombia and write in Venezuela, because the assets had very different business, legal, and technical requirements. Still this level of detail was a great time saver for Venezuela.

There were, then, benefits on different levels and during different phases of the project. Often what the team got the most benefit from was when the Knowledge Asset outlined the several options that the Colombia team had about a given issue and explained the reasons why Colombia chose one over another. In fact, as the Venezuela team members put their own plan together, they often chose a different option than Colombia had selected. It was not so much what Colombia did, but why they did it, that informed the thinking of the Venezuela team.

With this kind of assistance Steve's team got the job done in seven weeks and met its financial goals!

The pieces are in place for Strategic Transfer when a team has taken on a task that happens only infrequently—a one-off project—and wants to benefit from the experience of others, in other parts of the organization, that have done a similar task. Such projects involve strategic-level work, as the story about the Venezuela restructuring illustrates. Other examples of Strategic Transfer might be a product launch, an acquisition, or entry into a new country. The need for such tasks at a site is so infrequent that the knowledge from the last time may no longer be remembered or, as with the Venezuela restructuring, may never have been developed in a unit. Yet the knowledge does exist somewhere in the collective memory of the organization. It is Strategic Transfer that people are wishing for when they say, "We don't want to have to keep reinventing the wheel"; they believe that there are others, in other parts of the organization, that have gained knowledge that could be of great value to them as they start their task. It might, in fact, be worth millions of dollars if the next product launch or acquisition team could make use of what has been learned by other teams.

Strategic Transfer is like Far Transfer in that the transferred knowledge will most certainly have originated in a different geographic location, with a different culture, using a different technology, and with a different set of competitors. However, where Far Transfer impacts only a single team and the task it is doing, Strategic Transfer impacts large parts of the organization. The Venezuela restructuring in the example above impacted nearly every part of the Venezuela Asset.

Strategic Transfer is applicable when the collective knowledge (both tacit and explicit) of the organization is needed to accomplish a strategic task that occurs infrequently but is of critical importance to the whole organization.

EXAMPLES OF STRATEGIC TRANSFER

Of all the transfer categories I have discussed, this category presents organizations the most difficulty in building effective systems. I have, however, found examples that are highly effective and from which I draw the design guidelines: British Petroleum's Knowledge Assets and the U.S. Army's Center for Army Lessons Learned. I have also included the Learning History process as a viable method for Strategic Transfer. I start with BP's Knowledge Assets, elaborating on the example already provided.

BRITISH PETROLEUM—KNOWLEDGE ASSETS

I noted earlier that BP has a framework for thinking about knowledge management that includes learning before, learning during, and learning after. In the last chapter I identified Peer Assist as "learning before." In the chapter on Serial Transfer I identified AARs as "learning during," and in this chapter I describe the third process, "learning after."

BP's Knowledge Asset has gone through a lengthy evolution to reach its present form. Early on, BP created an unstructured knowledge repository that relied on a search engine for retrieval. However, it did not take long to discover that a repository was not effective for Strategic Transfer because those who needed the knowledge did not know what they did not know, which made the use of a search engine, no matter how sophisticated, ineffective. Over time the unstructured repository evolved into a structured repository, which was categorized by topic. This model still did not solve the difficulty of people being able to find only knowledge they were aware they needed. And the structured repository brought with it a new set of problems. First, any categorization framework that was developed became outdated quickly, so knowledge was frequently having to be resorted and reassigned to categories. In addition, different parts of the organization tended to use different names for what was often the same concept, so the same knowledge ended up being duplicated in several categories.

The repository has now evolved into a limited number of Knowledge Assets. A Knowledge Asset is BP's accumulated knowledge about a very specific topic that is prepackaged for an identified end user. Prepackaged means that a "knowledge specialist" has included in the asset those things that a team, relatively unfamiliar with the topic, would need to consider if it was assigned the task. In this way it differs significantly from Near Transfer, where the assumption is that the end user is very familiar with the topic. BP has developed Knowledge Assets for only a handful of topics, those that are of the greatest strategic significance to the company, for example, shift handovers, building a retail site, restructuring, entering new markets, refinery maintenance shutdown, and joint ventures.

The primary reason for limiting the use of this form of transfer is the large amount of time involved in developing a Knowledge Asset. Although the knowledge that goes into a Knowledge Asset draws on the experience of teams around the world, the teams are not themselves expected to package the knowledge for others. At BP that is the responsibility of members of the Central Knowledge Management team, who have developed special skills in compiling and packaging knowledge. These knowledge specialists travel to where a team that has important experience to share about one of these topics is located, to interview the team members. They collect documents, checklists, and tools that have been developed. Sometimes they even videotape team members or processes. Their goal is to synthesize the knowledge derived from multiple examples around the world.

The question the knowledge specialists ask is not "What has this team learned?" but "What does the end user need to know about this topic?" It turns out that is a very different question. The first focuses on the source, the second on the end user. A knowledge specialist may need to really probe team members to ferret out the reasoning behind their actions or to help them recall other options they considered before settling on a course of action. But it is this tacit knowledge that will be of greatest benefit to an end user. The sections of a Knowledge Asset include:

- **BUSINESS CONTEXT**—In this section the strategic intent is outlined. For example, the context of restructuring for BP might be to retain expertise in certain critical areas while reducing headcount. Having a context section is a recognition that all knowledge is based on certain assumptions that those attempting to employ the knowledge must take into consideration. Over time the context may change significantly, and then the other parts of the Knowledge Asset would need to change as well.

- **GUIDELINES**—This section contains the distilled wisdom or principles generalized from the many examples. Guidelines might be in the form of a checklist or a bulleted list.

- **LINKS TO PEOPLE**—The names and pictures of people who are knowledgeable about the topic and from whom further information could be obtained are provided. Hot links are established to facilitate contact.

- **PERFORMANCE HISTORIES**—These are the case histories from which the guidelines are drawn. They include stories and quotes that bring color and life to the Knowledge Asset. Often the performance histories include videos of those who were involved in the experience.

- **ARTIFACTS AND RECORDS OF RELEVANCE**—These include work products such as project plans, schedules, memos, and other items that users might be able to modify rather than reinvent.

The knowledge contained in a Knowledge Asset is a combination of the explicit knowledge found in the checklists and documents and the tacit knowledge lodged in the stories, quotes, reasoning, and examples. BP's goal in constructing a Knowledge Asset is not to make explicit everything that every team knows about the subject of that Knowledge Asset. A receiving team would need to get much of the needed tacit knowledge through in-depth phone conversations with knowledgeable people who have been identified in the Knowledge Asset or through inviting those colleagues to participate in a Peer Assist. What the Knowledge Asset is able to do is to raise issues that the receiving team may not have considered, to offer multiple perspectives on difficult issues, and to offer BP's collective experience on the topic.

After the Knowledge Asset has been constructed by knowledge specialists, it is turned over to a community of practice that has the responsibility for keeping it current.

U.S. Army—Center for Army Lessons Learned

Like most of the organizations I have written about in this book, the U.S. Army has been caught up in global change. The Army's main competitor, the Soviet Union, has disappeared. The Army's forces have been reduced by 500,000 and its budget cut by $40 billion. Even the mission of the Army has changed from being primarily about combat to increasingly being focused on peacekeeping. The elimination of the draft has significantly altered the type of personnel in the Army and has made both recruitment and retention issues significant. Recognizing all of these very critical factors, the Army has seen the need for both responding to and anticipating change. One of the main vehicles for that change effort has been CALL, the Center for Army Lessons Learned, located in Fort Leavenworth, Kansas. The mission of this "knowledge center" is to assemble, assimilate, and leverage the knowledge that the Army learns in the field. The four-step model on which CALL is based involves:

1. identifying learning opportunities,

2. observing and collecting knowledge,

3. creating knowledge products, and

4. deploying expertise.

The knowledge that CALL focuses on is identified by senior leaders of the Army. They determine what knowledge will be needed for the future and where holes and gaps exist in the Army's current knowledge. This proactive stance is a critical factor for the way CALL operates. The senior leaders are also able to identify *where* opportunities exist for gaining knowledge about the topics they have identified. For example, the 1994 peacekeeping mission in Haiti was identified as an opportunity for the Army to gain additional knowledge about peacekeeping.

Collectors were sent with the first troops that went into Haiti. These collectors were subject matter experts, "borrowed" from other parts of the Army, who included people with expertise in logistics, communications, linguistics, engineering, and supply. They were given training in how to be effective collectors of knowledge data. Their task was to look for answers to recurring problems rather than problems due to error or temporary anomalies. They collected multiple perspectives on each event, observing, interviewing, and taking digital photographs and video. They followed decisions that had been made to their outcomes and backward to discover the reasoning and logic that led to each decision. In so doing they teased out tacit as well as explicit knowledge. In Haiti, the twelve collectors assigned observed events as they occurred and recorded their descriptions in real time rather than retrospectively.

Daily the information they collected was sent back to CALL by Intranet. At CALL it was analyzed by yet another group of subject matter experts who were responsible for taking an enormous amount of disparate data from the multiple collectors and constructing new and useful knowledge out of it—theirs was a "sensemaking" task, to use Karl Weick's term.[1] They made preliminary interpretations, which they put on the Intranet for other knowledgeable professionals to comment on. Thus long before a final "lesson" was concluded, knowledge from the field had begun to move around the organization.

By the time the second wave of troops was sent into Haiti six months later, CALL had developed twenty-six scenarios of situations faced by the initial troops. These scenarios became a major training tool for their replacements. The scenarios included footage of actual events so that arriving troops were to some extent on familiar ground. They had, in a real sense, been there. They had seen the Haitians, heard the cadence of their voices, experienced the frustrations of the troops, and examined the terrain. They arrived knowing what they were facing and how to deal with it.

The knowledge generated in the Haiti mission produced other knowledge products and used other forms of distribution as well. For example, CALL also generated subject matter reports on topics such as the distribution and use of potable water, and how to better integrate Army and Air Force efforts.

At CALL the processes of collection, interpretation, and dissemination are intertwined rather than discrete or sequential. For example, at the same time the knowledge analysts at CALL were involved in interpreting the data, they were also helping to devise better questions for the collectors to ask in the field and were suggesting ways that the collectors might test their developing interpretations. It was a very dynamic process with ideas flowing in many directions. Even the collectors in the field functioned as both gatherers and disseminators. They assisted when extra hands were needed in an emergency and made an effort to improve the current operation on the ground by sharing solutions from their own experience and knowledge.

The "lessons" generated out of this complex and many-step process go through a final step where a "murder board" determines whether each lesson is important enough to be distributed. Finally, the knowledge is translated into many forms that amplify its reuse, the lessons become a part of Army doctrine, are made available as issues reports, become a key element in training, and are placed on the CALL web.

LEARNING HISTORIES

A learning history is a process, originally developed at MIT, to capture knowledge about how an organization learns. The principal researchers have been Art Kleiner and George Roth, whose most prominent history to date has been a product development effort at a major U.S. automobile company.[2] Although learning histories were not developed by a specific organization, I have included them as an example of Strategic Transfer because they are supported by a well-developed theory and are notable for having an exacting research protocol. Like the other examples in this section, they are a process for capturing usable knowledge from an extended experience of a team and transfering that knowledge to another team that may be distant in terms of context.

A learning history results in a narrative document, from twenty to a hundred pages in length, that describes an event in an organization's history. Most of the narrative is presented in a two-column format. The right-hand column is made up of quotes taken from interviews with participants in the experience. The quotes are not attributed, except by title (e.g., Senior Manager, Engineer, etc.), so a level of anonymity is afforded those involved. The quotes represent multiple views, sometimes offering contradictory perspectives on the same issue. The left-hand column is made up of comments on the quotes and questions that the quotes raised for the learning historians who constructed the narrative.

The whole narrative is divided into sections or stories each of which has a provocative title and begins with a prologue, which sets the context for the quotes that follow. The learning historians who select the quotes that are used to tell the story and who comment on what is happening in the narrative are a small team composed of outsiders, often academics and consultants, and insiders, often HR personnel, all of whom have been trained in the learning history technique. This team conducts and records interviews during the time period of the event, rather than retrospectively.

Learning histories involve a process to transfer the knowledge as well as processes to collect and document it. The process used to transfer the knowledge to a different team that may be able to use it is for the receiving team members to read the narrative and mark passages that raise questions for them. The receiving team then meets to hold in-depth conversations about the learning history. Out of these discussions the group creates the meaning that will guide its own action. Kleiner and Roth see learning histories as both process and product: the process the receiving team engages in as it reads, critiques, and discusses the learning history is a key element of the transfer process.

An example of a learning history is a breakthrough made by a team in an oil refinery in the Midwest. This cross-functional team developed a new maintenance strategy that saved the refinery $1.5 million. The learning history document detailed how the new strategy was developed and why. But when the twenty-page document was distributed to the six hundred other employees of the refinery and to other refineries within the organization, it sent a more important message: that innovative solutions can be forged internally. As reported by a manager of the oil company, "The learning history was extremely important to our proactive manufacturing effort. It was a way for everyone—

operators and managers alike—to recognize that a more proactive manufacturing approach has a shot, and maybe they should
contribute to it. For the next two years, we referred back to the
learning history at key moments. And we generated 150 more
such innovations at the refinery."[3] Kleiner and Roth outline seven
steps in a learning history project:

1. **PLANNING**—In this step team members are selected and the
    scope of the project, including the specific questions the
    history is to deal with, is identified.

2. **REFLECTIVE RESEARCH**—Interviews are conducted by both the
    internal and external historians, who also observe action
    and examine documents. Interviewers may conduct between
    fifty and one hundred interviews, including outsiders (suppli-
    ers and consultants).

3. **DISTILLATION**—The team of learning historians synthesizes
    the data from the interviews, observations, field notes, and
    documents into themes that have two characteristics: they
    are supported by the data and they tell a compelling story
    that will have meaning to others in the organization.

4. **WRITING**—A document is produced that is a "jointly told
    tale," that is, it uses the voices of the participants and the
    broader perspective of the learning historians. That broader
    perspective may include insights from organizational litera-
    ture or from other organizations.

5. **VALIDATION**—This step allows those quoted to review what
    they have said and to correct or modify it. In this way it is
    not only a validation but also a reconsideration that may
    add new insights both for the document and for the actors
    in the event. This step also involves bringing together small
    groups of participants who can test the writing for usefulness
    to the larger community.

6. **DISSEMINATION**—Rather than being handed out as a report,
    the final document is provided to representatives from across
    the organization in a workshop format. Participants are

asked to discuss such questions as "How typical was this story?" and "How can the knowledge increase your own capabilities?" The intent of this step is to transfer the knowledge from the originating team to the whole organization.

7. **PUBLICATION/OUTREACH**—The learning history is made available to audiences beyond the originating organization through journal articles and conference presentations. The anonymity of the originating organization is preserved in this process.[4]

As the seven steps illustrate, creating a learning history is labor-intensive and can be expensive. But as the seven steps also illustrate, effective Strategic Transfer involves much more than creating a report of what happened.

It is important to build systems for Strategic Transfer, of whatever type, when that is the only way that knowledge can be transferred, certainly not when the less costly processes for Serial or Near Transfer can suffice. The questions that follow are critical in making that determination.

CRITERIA RELATED TO STRATEGIC TRANSFER

To illustrate the criteria for Strategic Transfer, I will return to the first example provided in this chapter, BP's Knowledge Asset for restructuring, and use it to illustrate the factors that necessitate the use of the guidelines for Strategic Transfer.

1. Who the intended receiver of the knowledge is in terms of similarity of task and context

QUESTIONS	ANSWERS FOR TRANSFER BETWEEN RESTRUCTURING TEAMS
How similar are the task and the context of the receiving team(s) to those of the source team?	Both the source team and the receiving team are dealing with the task of restructuring, but for each team that takes place in a different context with differing political, legal, technological, and environmental considerations.

Does the receiving team(s) have the absorptive capacity (experience, technical knowledge, shared language) to implement what the source team has developed?

The absorptive capacity of the receiving team is likely to be weak because it has not done the task of restructuring before. Multiple examples, detailed reasoning, and multiple options will be needed to address the lack of absorptive capacity. In other words, the Knowledge Asset may need to speak to varying levels of capacity.

2. How routine and frequent the task is

QUESTIONS	ANSWERS FOR TRANSFER BETWEEN RESTRUCTURING TEAMS
How frequently does this task occur? Daily? Monthly? Yearly?	The task of restructuring is done infrequently in an organizational unit. There may be no one on the team who has done the task before. However, across the organization and over time the task will be repeated, and therefore the knowledge needs to be transferred.
Is the task routine or nonroutine? Are there clear steps, or is each next step variable?	The task is nonroutine. A restructuring would never be done the same way twice. Every site is different, presenting its own unique characteristics.

3. The kind of knowledge that is being transferred

QUESTIONS	ANSWERS FOR TRANSFER BETWEEN RESTRUCTURING TEAMS
Is the knowledge of the source team primarily tacit or explicit?	Both tacit and explicit knowledge are involved, and both are critical to successful transfer.
How many functional areas of the organization will be impacted by implementing the	All parts of the system are impacted by the knowledge of the restructuring team. The impact is far reaching and long lasting. The new actions

knowledge? One team? One division? The whole organization? of the team will require changes in the behavior of people, as well as changes in processes or technical actions. It involves goals as well as the means to reach those goals. People in the organization have to think of themselves in new ways or in new relationships with the organization.

DESIGN GUIDELINES FOR STRATEGIC TRANSFER

A conventional answer to the question "How can you accomplish Strategic Transfer?" would be "Translate the specifics of a situation into more generalized principles." Each of the examples I have offered does, in fact, incorporate general principles; they are one element of BP's Knowledge Assets, they are found in the left-hand column of learning histories, and they become a part of Army doctrine for CALL. But in none of these examples do principles stand by themselves. Principles as stand-alone items are too general to be of much help to anyone. As one of the engineers at BP told me, "When I go into a database and read something like 'First, you have to get your priorities straight,' I understand that those words must have had great meaning to the group that wrote them, but I find them thoroughly unhelpful."

The guidelines for Strategic Transfer list the design elements that need to be in place in order to make this kind of transfer work. These guidelines are an attempt to avoid two common errors: first, having nothing more than a list of principles that are too generalized to be useful; second, having so much detail and information that no one would ever go through it all.

KNOWLEDGE NEEDED IS IDENTIFIED BY SENIOR-LEVEL MANAGERS

Strategic Transfer is forward looking. Where the other transfer processes that I have described have asked, "What knowledge do we have that we can leverage?" this transfer process asks,

"What knowledge do we need?" Because this question is asked in terms of the future direction and mission of the company, it is up to those in senior-level roles to identify the topics about which the organization should proactively seek knowledge. Strategic Transfer is used when the assumption is made that the needed knowledge *does* exist somewhere in the organization, although it may be widely dispersed. Or if the needed topic is new to the organization, the assumption is made that viable knowledge can be extracted from the ongoing experience of teams who are currently engaged in addressing the task. In either instance, it is not external knowledge that is sought but knowledge that resides within the organization's collective memory. Senior leaders' responsibility is to direct the company's resources to the task of synthesizing what is known. This responsibility is illustrated both in the BP example of the Knowledge Asset and in the U.S. Army description of CALL. In both examples senior leaders have identified areas that have high potential for generating knowledge that has future strategic value. Because of the time and cost commitment involved in Strategic Transfer, only a limited number of areas can be addressed and the choice of topics is significant.

A second critical task of this senior group is the identification of *where* the opportunities are for collecting this knowledge. BP's leaders would know, for example, where restructuring may be happening next or when a proposed acquisition is an opportunity to construct knowledge. Such opportunities, as the Haiti example illustrates, do not have to be identified as "best" but only as occasions where it is possible to learn from the experience—what the Army calls gaining "ground truth."

KNOWLEDGE SPECIALISTS COLLECT AND INTERPRET THE KNOWLEDGE

For Near Transfer those who live the experience write it up, as in the TI Alert Notification example. Not so for Strategic Transfer. Although the team members involved in the experience are a primary source of knowledge, they are not the people responsible for making it usable for others. As figure 2–3 in chapter 2 shows, the step of translating knowledge into a form usable by others is separate from developing common knowledge for the team's own use. That first step is important for any group to function more effectively. But the knowledge that a group constructs for Serial Transfer would have to go through a translation process to make it usable by other teams. In fact, Army collectors do often sit in on AARs in the location where they are collecting. But the data gleaned from such meetings is only a small part of a larger data set used to find answers to the questions they are addressing. As Nick Milton, one of BP's knowledge specialists, has noted, "We do not rely on people populating the knowledge banks themselves, as experience has shown us that you end up only with the superficial knowledge, never the real deep knowledge—never the voice of experience."[5]

In all three examples of Strategic Transfer that I have provided here, nonteam members have done the collecting and synthesis of the experience. BP relies on members of the Central Knowledge Management Team, the learning history process uses a team of internal and external members trained as learning historians, and the U.S. Army uses collectors. For convenience, I will reference all of these people as "knowledge specialists."

To collect knowledge from teams, knowledge specialists need a set of skills that enable them to formulate questions that elicit the reasoning of each person being interviewed. They need the ability to recognize inferences that others make and to frame questions that test those inferences.[6] This questioning ability is enhanced by the knowledge specialists' coming from outside the frame of reference of those who are engaged in the action, because it is harder to recognize as inferences those biases that we share with others. The development of these skills, which are critical for translating experience into knowledge, requires considerable training and preparation. It is also helpful for the knowledge specialists to have some measure of subject matter expertise.

CALL borrows people who are well experienced in the subject matter and then brings them to Fort Leavenworth for up to eight weeks of training to learn the skills of data collection. CALL looks for people who can quickly build their credibility and rapport, yet are able to maintain emotional distance. In addition, CALL wants collectors who have large networks they can call on for information and support. Borrowing personnel from other units has the added advantage of facilitating the dissemination of the new knowledge that is being developed, because when these experts return to their own units they take back with them the knowledge they gained on location. CALL works with each member of the collector team to "develop customized 'directed telescope' collection plans, consisting of hierarchical levels of questions focused on each area of expertise. Each item on the list is expanded into increasingly detailed sets of questions around events members expect to observe in the field."[7] These collectors have not come along with the troops to pick up what they can—they are targeting specific knowledge areas.

A member of BP's central knowledge management team spent a lengthy period of time in Colombia interviewing and constructing much of the knowledge and interpretation that became the Restructuring Knowledge Asset. As the earlier story illustrates, the Venezuela change team members found this Knowledge Asset of considerable help. They recognized that without it they might have not been able to meet the ambitious time line they had been given. Yet when I asked the Venezuela team leader how they were planning to add to the Knowledge Asset, he said he was unsure as to whether they even would. Their own experience had made them conscious of the great difference between the kind of end-of-project report they knew how to write and the more useful and sophisticated Knowledge Asset of which they had just made use. Without considerable assistance from someone more experienced in knowledge construction than they were, they feared that any report they constructed would be of little use to others.

I mentioned earlier that it was helpful for those doing the collecting to come from outside the team because of the perspective they bring. External perspective is helpful in a second way, in that it reduces both the actual and the perceived bias of those collecting the data. It reduces actual bias because the process of collecting data is also a part of the sensemaking process. What final sense is made of the data is impacted by *who* is considered a viable source of knowledge on a topic, *what topics* are addressed and which are slighted, and which areas are pursued *in-depth* and which are pursued only superficially. Using knowledge specialists, who are not members of the team involved in the task, to make these data collection choices is a safeguard that helps to control data collection bias. If a team were attempting to collect data on itself, team members might be inclined to give greater weight to the interpretations of those who had more political clout or to be influenced by concerns of retribution or reward.

Using nonmembers to collect data about a team's experience reduces *perceived* bias in that recipients of the knowledge can be somewhat suspicious of groups that tout their own accomplishments. Thus one considerable advantage of engaging nonmembers in interviewing, observation, and sensemaking is the increased believability of the resulting knowledge.

I have said less in this section about the use of nonmembers to analyze and synthesize the data collected, which is equally critical to Strategic Transfer. I will elaborate on that factor in "Multiple Voices Are Synthesized," below.

COLLECTION OCCURS IN REAL TIME RATHER THAN RETROSPECTIVELY

It is not always possible to collect and construct knowledge in real time, but when it is possible, a great deal more is learned than when team members rely on their memory of past events and reasoning. We are all great historical revisionists. As we learn and change, we revise the past in terms of our present understanding. It is not so much that the remembered facts change, as it is that we change which facts we give prominence. Our memories are selective; both collectively and individually we remember the events that support the final outcome and allow other events to fade into obscurity. Our interpretation of the facts changes as well. It is, after all, not just the facts that matter but also how we put them together and what conclusions we draw from them—in other words, our reasoning. As Karl Weick notes:

> The basic finding that investigators keep returning to . . . is that people who know the outcome of a complex prior history

of tangled, indeterminate events remember that history as being much more determinant, leading "inevitably" to the outcome they already knew. Furthermore, the nature of these determinant histories is reconstructed differently, depending on whether the outcomes are seen as good or bad. If the outcome is perceived to be bad, then antecedents are reconstructed to emphasize incorrect actions, flawed analyses, and inaccurate perceptions, even if such flaws were not influential or all that obvious at the time. . . . Thus, hindsight both tightens causal couplings and reconstructs as coupled events a history that leads directly to the outcome.[8]

As the Haiti example illustrates, CALL develops its knowledge out of real-time events. The collectors do not interview unit personnel about *what happened* but observe what *is happening*, and interview those involved about their reasoning and understanding of the situation. And "being there" allows the collectors to capture the reality of the situation on video and in digital pictures rather than reporting someone's remembrance of the sights, sounds, and emotions that were present.

Likewise, learning historians see a need to be present at events. They sit in on meetings and observe discussions. They interview those involved about their current understanding of the events, often capturing their verbatim language. They probe those they interview for insight into their assumptions and reasoning. Over time they are able to capture not only what happened but how the thinking about what was happening changed.

In both of these situations, the interview questions may influence what is happening. However, in neither situation is there an attempt to keep data collection and organizational understanding separate, as one might aim for in a traditional research study. In fact, the CALL collectors are charged with adding what knowledge they can to improve the situation. Likewise the learning historians see the interviews as building "reflective capacity" within the organization.

FOCUS IS ON THE END USER

Earlier I suggested that Strategic Transfer was about the future rather than the past, and that it was in that way different from the other transfer categories. I want to suggest yet another way in which Strategic Transfer differs from the other categories: it is focused on the end user, or the recipient of the knowledge, rather than the source.

Uncovering what the end user will need is no easy task because those who will be receiving the knowledge are unlikely to know what they will need. So it is not particularly helpful to say to them, "What do you need to know about this topic?" What they most need is, in fact, what they are most unaware that they need. On the other hand, those who have been involved in the task are often so familiar with it that they can no longer say what knowledge is necessary to do the task. It seems that neither end of this transfer process is able to specify what is needed. It falls to knowledge specialists to ascertain what the end user will need, and to develop the knowledge and the format based on those needs.

For CALL, having a customer focus means having not one but multiple knowledge products that target different customers. The knowledge that CALL develops is (1) made available as training in the form of scenarios or simulations, (2) incorporated into Army doctrine, (3) placed on the Intranet in the Lessons Learned database, (4) immediately returned to the field as answers to questions, (5) used to develop reports for specialized units, and (6) used as custom-designed responses to critical questions asked by senior leaders. Thus the knowledge is not "stored" in the sense that the term usually implies, that is, in a static or stable form. Rather, it is held in a way that allows it to be continually reconfigured and reanalyzed as new needs arise.

CALL also keeps its customer focus by employing a broad network of people to help determine what questions the collectors need to ask. Once collectors have been identified and trained for a specific engagement, they each develop yet more specific areas to investigate through talking with commanders before the action begins and by talking with their own extensive networks about the specific areas in which knowledge needs to be extended. Using this wide network, the collectors expand and refine both the questions to ask and the topics that others see as needful.

For BP, "customer-focused" means that the Knowledge Asset incorporates multiple types of assistance in multiple formats, including advice about the project, help in making decisions, the BP context, an awareness of what the knowledge is based on so users can determine the extent to which they can trust the material, stories and quotes that make the knowledge come alive, and ways for users to follow up on what they are learning. This multilayered approach allowed BP's Venezuela team to obtain different knowledge at different time periods during its project. First it needed to understand what it might be missing and it wanted a confirmation that it was on the right track. It was only later in the work that it sought out details about HR plans and schedules.

John Seely Brown and Paul Duguid provide a useful analogy of what it means to make local knowledge of benefit to a broader group.[9] They compare developing useful knowledge to the way a production company takes a story idea and stage by stage develops it into a movie. In a movie we are interested in what happened but equally we want to know why it happened and what meaning it had to the major characters. The movie analogy invokes a sense of transforming knowledge, of making it more intelligible, and of making it more palatable.

MULTIPLE VOICES ARE SYNTHESIZED

The philosopher John Stuart Mill said, "Since the general or prevailing opinion on any subject is rarely or never the whole truth, it is only by the collision of adverse opinion that the remainder of the truth has any chance of being supplied." And while I might hesitate to label the kind of organizational knowledge I have been discussing here as "truth," Mill's observation nevertheless speaks to an important issue: the need for "requisite variety."

Since the knowledge of Strategic Transfer is complex, the challenge is to construct a method of transfer that accommodates the level of complexity that occurs in such actions as peacekeeping missions, mergers, and product development. In keeping with cyberneticists Roger Conant and Robert Ashby's concept that "the variety within a system must be at least as great as the environmental variety against which it is attempting to regulate itself," we can assume that Strategic Transfer will have to maintain the variety within the inputs.[10] The challenge, then, is how to "make sense" of the knowledge gained from complex experiences without losing the multiple voices from multiple examples. It is clear that reducing the complexity to a simple solution or steps of process, which worked for Near Transfer, is not sufficient here.

In each of the examples I have given of Strategic Transfer, there is a bringing together of differing opinions, whether through the use of eight or ten different collectors and multiple interpreters for CALL, or by learning historians interviewing people of varying levels and positions about the same issue. This confluence of voices seems critical to the development of useful complex knowledge. Kleiner and Roth suggest, "Each point of view represents a valid, but limited, piece of the solution to the puzzle. If all these perspectives could be integrated coherently, the organization as a whole might learn what happened, why it happened, and what to do next."[11]

For CALL, the synthesis of multiple voices involves not only having multiple collectors in multiple sites but also having multiple analysts to receive data from the field work and make sense of it. To assist them in that sensemaking the analysts send their tentative interpretations out to a larger network to get feedback that will add to their interpretation.

This availability of multiple voices in BP's Restructuring Asset made it exceptionally helpful to the Venezuela change team. The members were very aware that the restructuring they were responsible for in Venezuela was very different from the Colombia situation. In fact, at times the difference was of use to them in comparing an option they chose to one Colombia had chosen for a particular action. As one Venezuela team member said, "People gave different reasons behind why something was done or why one option was selected over another. It is helpful to hear the different reasons."

What I am suggesting is quite different from the idea of developing a database that holds many submissions each of which offers an alternative method of accomplishing a task or project. What is necessary for Strategic Transfer is some form of interpretation that blends the many voices without losing them. The multiple inputs are used to create a synthesis of knowledge but also to illustrate, amplify, verify, and continually challenge it.

Business Driver

The business driver for Strategic Transfer is the need to reduce the costs and time involved in reinventing solutions to strategic issues. This is particularly important in large multinational companies where the same issue is likely to arise in different parts of the world over extended periods of time. The topics that are the subject of Strategic Transfer are those that often have long-lasting and wide impact, so the ability to bring to bear all of the organization's knowledge on such issues has long been a sought-after target that only recently seems possible.

Barriers and Problems

The barriers to Strategic Transfer are related to logistics, such as limits on time and personnel, and mind-set—that is, the ingrained practice of having team members themselves write the report on what they learned. The concerns people raise about Strategic Transfer typically touch on both of these issues.

It's Too Expensive to Have a Group of Knowledge Specialists

One of the clever ways that CALL has handled the issue of cost for Strategic Transfer is to use people on a temporary basis who are borrowed from other units. Not only does this reduce the cost of collecting the data, but it serves as a critical step in the dissemination process as well. But part of the issue, I think, is not the actual cost, but the perceived cost. If learning historians or members of a central management team or even Army collectors come into a unit to observe and ask questions, others identify them as dedicated to a knowledge task and recognize that as a new type of cost that the company is incurring, that is, it is perceived as expensive. However, the visibility of the knowledge specialists also has a positive side in that it highlights the organization's interest in sharing knowledge.

But the collection process is not the only cost of Strategic Transfer; there also have to be people available who can synthesize the data and who have the skills to develop knowledge products out of what has been learned. This is a larger and more sophisticated task than members of a community of practice or people on temporary assignment can take on. It requires personnel, if not dedicated to the task, at least with the expertise and committed time to build sophisticated products. For this reason it only makes sense to do Strategic Transfer when the leadership of the organization believes the specific knowledge is critical to the organization's future. Clearly, knowledge that would keep a merger from failing or that would make a product launch more successful reaches that level of need.

One important way to reduce cost is to use the processes described for Strategic Transfer only when the knowledge meets the criteria outlined earlier. For other kinds of transfer, less costly processes should be used. Making this differentiation not only saves costs, it increases the effectiveness of the transfer process as well.

If the Company Identifies a "Way to Do Something" We Will All Have to Conform

As more companies experiment with knowledge sharing, the concern that there will be a requirement for units to conform to a company-sanctioned "best practice" becomes more worrisome to organizational members. The intent of Strategic Transfer is to inform without dictating, but what starts out as "informing" can too easily turn into "dictating." I want to suggest two safeguards, neither of which may totally resolve this concern.

The first safeguard is to make conspicuous the principles on which knowledge sharing is based. When an organization decides to be proactive about sharing knowledge, the way the idea is "sold" is usually to talk about potential gains in productivity— and rightly so. But it is equally important that the sales pitch speak to the principles on which the sharing will be based. And those principles need to have been carefully thought through ahead of time. As an example of articulating the principles, John Browne, the CEO of BP, talks about knowledge sharing as making connections between people. And true to that principle, BP has created such processes as AARs , Peer Assists, and virtual teaming through videoconferencing as the primary ways it moves knowledge. BP employees even joke that they "bring knowledge in, in bags of skin." If there is an articulated philosophy about "informing without dictating" or about "improving upon what others have developed," that principle sets a tone that can prevent later interpretations that can unwittingly run counter to the intended goal of the knowledge sharing.

The second safeguard is to build into the knowledge products multiple voices representing multiple options. When multiple voices and challenges are present, it is less likely that "one way" will become required. Multiple voices may be available through multiple case histories, each of which offers the experience of a different unit with its own unique set of circumstances. Or multiple voices may be offered by having knowledge specialists custom design a knowledge product for a "client" based on the client's unique circumstances. Or multiple voices may be available by including in case histories both what worked and what did not work in a unit's experience. All of these ways and more indicate to users that there is not just one way to do a refinery shutdown or to enter a new country.

Summary

Strategic Transfer is applicable when the tacit and explicit collective knowledge of the organization, related to a strategic task that occurs infrequently, is made available to a team that has been assigned to carry out that task for a unit. Nick Milton talks about the need to extend the "shelf life" of strategic knowledge.[12] That is what Strategic Transfer accomplishes by making available to the organization knowledge that otherwise would be lost or forgotten.

Strategic Transfer deals with both explicit and tacit knowl-

TABLE 6-1

DESIGN GUIDELINES FOR STRATEGIC TRANSFER

Definition	The collective knowledge of the organization is needed to accomplish a strategic task that occurs infrequently but is critical to the whole organization.
Similarity of task and context	The receiving team does a task that impacts the whole organization in a context different from that of the source team.
Nature of the task	Infrequent and nonroutine
Type of knowledge	Tacit and explicit
Design guidelines	Knowledge needed is identified by senior-level managers
	Knowledge specialists collect and interpret the knowledge
	Collection occurs in real time rather than retrospectively
	Focus is on the end user
	Multiple voices are synthesized
Example	A company acquires ABC; six months later another team in a different location uses what was learned with ABC to acquire DFG.

edge. The tasks involved are so complex and so far reaching that the transfer mechanism cannot fully provide either. Any explicit knowledge offered has to be modified and added to in order to accomplish the task of the receiving team. Any tacit knowledge must be augmented through person-to-person conversations. Often the Strategic Transfer mechanism can only point to a source or a need for further tacit knowledge.

Table 6–1 lists the design guidelines for Strategic Transfer. This type of transfer is unique in several ways: it is forward looking, developing needed knowledge rather than taking advantage of existing knowledge; it impacts multiple units of an organization rather than only one team; and the focus is on the end user rather than on the source.

The next chapter, "Expert Transfer," completes the five types of transfer.

CHAPTER 7

EXPERT TRANSFER

Buckman Labs' general manager in Asia, Dennis Dalton, was putting together a proposal for pitch control that he was going to submit to a prospective client, an Indonesian pulp mill. Pitch occurs in both hard and soft woods and must be washed out by some type of enzyme and other dispersants in the process of turning wood into pulp for making cardboard and paper. The difficulty is that the pitch differs depending on the species of tree. The pitch content even differs in coastal wood and tropical wood, so each pulp mill has to find the chemistry and process that works with the type of wood it is using. If the pitch is not adequately removed, the pulp will be spotty or slimy.

Dennis wanted to sell the Indonesian plant on a Buckman product and process that would reduce the number of pitch particles it was currently getting and reduce its pitch control costs as well. He had already done a good deal of thinking about the proposal he wanted to make, but he hoped to strengthen it by being able to show Buckman's expertise in places around the world. So in January he sent out a request over the Pulp and Paper Techforum:

> *We will be proposing a pitch control program to an Indonesian pulp mill that produces 1700 to 2000 tons per day of bleached pulp from mixed tropical hardwoods. We have already proposed that cost-performance be evaluated on a cost-per-ton-of-pulp basis, rather than comparing price per kilo of chemical. This will allow full utilization of our entire range of pitch control products to achieve optimum performance, rather than being locked in to one product. I would appreciate an update on successful recent pitch control strategies and/or long-running programs in your parts of the world, which we may want to consider for this Indonesian mill. Thanks for your help.*

Dennis got two replies the very next day and over the next two weeks got a total of eleven answers. The answers came from around the world, including Sweden, British Columbia, New Zealand, and Mexico. Some offered resources such as knowledgeable people to contact or a master's thesis on the topic; some specified particular chemicals that they had been testing recently and offered the results they had achieved; many attached detailed documents to their replies. Almost all ended their responses with good wishes and invitations to "give a call" if more detail or information was needed.

Dennis incorporated many of the responses into his proposal, and the Indonesian mill bought Buckman's product. From Dennis's perspective it was the speed of the response to his request that made the difference in winning the sale.

When Anita Kirkman, the lead sysop for the Pulp and Paper Techforum, thought all the responses were in, she received a summary from the section leader, put in the keywords for search, and filed the "thread." Ultimately, the answers benefited not only Dennis's project but a number of other pitch control programs.

Expert Transfer is applicable when teams facing an unusual technical problem beyond the scope of their own knowledge seek the expertise of others in the organization to help them address it. Typically, the knowledge that is requested is not found in a manual or in standard documentation. It may, for example, relate to outdated equipment, so only those who have been around a while know the answer; or maybe it relates to a new process that has just been introduced; or it may relate to a very specialized problem that would occur only under unusual circumstances. Even when the knowledge is obscure, the knowledge requested through Expert Transfer has a known, explicit answer. The knowledge is not a matter of interpretation, as it is with Far Transfer, or of having to develop the knowledge, as it often is with Strategic Transfer.

Technical expertise in an organization is a scarce and costly commodity, so Expert Transfer has become a convenient and workable way to share expertise that may be located anywhere in the world. Increasingly sophisticated technology makes it possible for teams to get an answer back for even the most obscure technical questions—somewhere around the world, someone will know the answer.

Electronic systems primarily facilitate the transfer of explicit knowledge. The messages are brief and to the point, making a request for very specific information.

EXAMPLES OF EXPERT TRANSFER

I have provided three examples of Expert Transfer: Buckman Laboratories Techforums, Tandem Computer's Second-Class Mail, and Chevron's Best Practices Resource Map.

BUCKMAN LABS—TECHFORUMS

One of the earliest attempts to share knowledge was Buckman Laboratories' Techforums, which started in 1992. Techforums are electronic discussion groups, primarily of the "Does anybody know. . . ?" type. There are twenty-four sections of Buckman's Techforums, most organized by industry group (e.g., pulp and paper, leather, etc.). Close to half of Buckman's employees have asked questions over the forums. Fewer, perhaps

10 to 20 percent, have responded to the questions others have asked, and of course an unknown number of people have been content to "lurk," reading and benefiting from what others have asked or offered. The reason for such a high rate of participation is the care Buckman takes to monitor and support the forums.

Each section of the forums has a section leader, who is responsible for either answering an inquiry or forwarding it to someone who can. Each section is also monitored by a professional library staff and sysops (system operators who are responsible for the maintenance of the forums). The library staff reads all of the messages and takes the initiative to respond to those that can be answered with library resources. However, if after twenty-four hours an inquiry has not received a response from the library or another Buckman associate, a sysop forwards the query to the section leader, who must find someone who can respond.

The section leader is also responsible for writing an abstract of the "thread" (the messages that make up a particular topic) once a particular discussion seems finished. Again, a librarian assumes responsibility for noting that a thread has finished and sending the pertinent items to the section leader. These finished abstracts (with keywords) are archived in the Techforum library.

In an effort to make the Techforums effective for knowledge transfer, Buckman Laboratories has gone far beyond simply making electronic space available. For example, when sales/field personnel complained that they did not have time to read numerous messages, the librarians undertook to construct a weekly summary of the exchanges in each section of the Techforum. This provided a briefer alternative for users wanting to access the knowledge that was being shared.

Other forums were established to fill other knowledge-sharing needs. Three forums were created to accommodate different language groups and to bridge cultural differences. The Foro Latino is primarily Spanish and Portuguese while the Euroforum is English, French, and German. The only regional forum, AAA, includes South Africa, Australia, and Asia. These forums have proven helpful in getting non–North American associates familiar and comfortable with an electronic environment, so much so that there now seems less need for these special language forums and they are being merged back into the Techforum.

One of the early success factors of the Techforum was the virtual presence of Bob Buckman, the CEO, who would often ask or respond to a question, or would occasionally mention to an employee that he had not noticed her or his presence in the Techforum lately.

TANDEM—SECOND-CLASS MAIL

In 1996, Tandem Computers (now a division of Compaq) employed eleven thousand people worldwide, almost all of whom made use of e-mail. At Tandem e-mail was organized into three classes: first-class mail was for person-to-person messages; second-class mail was for work-related messages that went to the entire organization, including headquarters announcements and industry news as well as requests for information; third-class mail was for extracurricular announcements or queries.

Researchers David Constant, Lee Sproull, and Sara Kiesler conducted a study of Tandem's second-class mail, in particular the 30 percent of that mail that contained requests.[1] The researchers were privy to the questions that were broadcast as well as the replies that were given. Moreover, they were able to query both the askers and the responders in an attempt to understand the motivation behind both kinds of acts. The system had been in place for six years at the time of the study and thus Tandem had a lengthy history of exchange.

The researchers discovered that people did not ask questions lightly or carelessly over the network. Almost all (91 percent) of those who broadcast questions had already made an attempt to get the information from other sources. The seekers resorted to the "Does anybody know . . . ?" format only when their normal collegial sources of information did not provide the needed answer.

The questions that were asked primarily sought technical information. For example, a typical question was:

> I am sure I'm not the first to ask this question but I can find
> no help in Quest [online database of previous public questions

and replies] so I'm copying the world to see if I can get any answers.

I have a number of 2311s [computer terminals] (50+) installed at ABC Co. and many of them are starting to get too dim even at the max brightness setting. Is there any way to increase the brightness of these monitors or is the solution a replacement? Any info would be greatly appreciated.

Notably, the questions asked were not political or strategic in nature. Seekers did not ask, for example, "Who do you think will be the next chief of engineering?" or "How can I get the purchasing department to respond quicker?" They were asking for explicit, technical knowledge. The seekers received an average of 7.8 replies per question. Some of the replies directly answered the question asked and some provided information that was useful to the seekers, such as other sources to try. Both kinds of information were considered useful by the seekers. Redundant replies were welcome in that they served as a kind of validation for answers.

When people think about electronic discussion forums, they often wonder why anyone would take the time to reply when there is no obvious benefit to the responder. On the other hand, no one much wonders why someone would offer assistance to an officemate or a long-time acquaintance. Our curiosity is more about why people help others with whom they have what the literature calls "weak ties." Why do they take time from their busy schedules to respond to someone they haven't met? The responders at Tandem spent an average of nine minutes per reply, which is a considerable investment to make for someone who is a stranger. Moreover, when the responders were asked how many other people they thought might have also responded to the same question, on average they estimated as many as fourteen people. Thus, they did not view themselves as the only source of knowledge about the topic and realized that their response might be redundant. All of which makes the question of why they help even more puzzling.

The answer that Constant et al. found was that positive regard for the organization was the primary reason people responded to others' queries. When asked, "Why did you answer this question?" the largest number of responders gave reasons related to general organizational benefit: "Answering questions like this is part of being a good company citizen," for example. Far fewer offered personal reasons, such as "I enjoy solving problems" or "I enjoy earning respect." And what is even more interesting, the responses of the people who were motivated by positive regard for the organization were rated as more useful by the person who had originally asked the question!

CHEVRON—BEST PRACTICES RESOURCE MAP

One of Chevron's early knowledge management activities was constructing a Best Practices Resource Map. In its original version the map was printed to look and fold like a road map, an apt symbol for an oil company. Over five thousand copies were distributed. The map is designed to help organizational members find their way to knowledge resources within Chevron. It identifies networks throughout Chevron, which have been categorized by the Baldrige categories. Each node (area of focus) on the map includes the name of the group and information about how it communicates (e.g., four to six meetings per year, Lotus Notes) as well as the name of a contact person and an e-mail address. The networks are quite varied; some use e-mail, others hold periodic meetings and conferences.

After the map was first printed and distributed, it quickly became evident that it was going to have to be constantly altered due to new links and revisions. So the map was placed on the Intranet and hot-linked to e-mail for instant contact. The map is now more widely accessible across Chevron and additional web resources for the networks can be linked directly to the map. Access to the nodes depends on the security of each node; for some, the user must make a request for access.

Chevron has gained considerable mileage out of the "knowledge map." Internally it serves as a visible and useful reminder of knowledge management, an area that is otherwise largely invisible to members. And externally it has been a visible sign of Chevron's leadership in the area of knowledge management.

Many other companies have built similar maps, Hughes Space and Communications has a Knowledge Highway that helps people locate knowledge within the organization. BP has a network of home pages it calls Connect. Assistance is offered in developing the home pages, but individuals are free to enter whatever information they think will be useful to others. This kind of resource is often called "yellow pages," and most often connects individuals rather than groups as Chevron's map does.

These electronic systems are carriers of explicit knowledge, as the Constant et al. study showed. But they can also serve as locators of the people who have the tacit knowledge that a team is seeking. Frequently, askers locate someone through Buckman Labs' Techforum or Chevron's Best Practices Resource Map and then connect face-to-face or through in-depth phone conversations to begin to gain the tacit knowledge they require.

TRANSFER CRITERIA RELATED TO EXPERT TRANSFER

To illustrate the criteria and guidelines for Expert Transfer, I again turn to Buckman Labs' Techforums.

1. Who the intended receiver of the knowledge is in terms of similarity of task and context

QUESTIONS	ANSWERS FOR TRANSFER BETWEEN PULP TEAMS
How similar are the task and the context of the receiving team(s) to those of the source team?	The receiving team was in Indonesia and the sources were from across the globe. All were, however, involved in pitch control, so the context was familiar if not similar. The specific task was developing a proposal with the latest knowledge, so for each team the task was different.
Does the receiving team(s) have the absorptive capacity (experience, technical	The language of the receiving team's request is filled with technical terms, but the source teams know the technical language and need no explana-

knowledge, shared language) to implement what the source team has developed?

tion to respond. The absorptive capacity of the receiving team is high.

2. How routine and frequent the task is

Questions	Answers for Transfer between Pulp Teams
How frequently does this task occur? Daily? Monthly? Yearly?	The task of writing a proposal to a plant for new business occurs with some frequency, albeit monthly rather than daily.
Is the task routine or nonroutine? Are there clear steps, or is each next step variable?	The task is nonroutine. Writing a proposal is different each time. Each plant is different and the technology continues to change.

3. The kind of knowledge that is being transferred

Questions	Answers for Transfer between Pulp Teams
Is the knowledge of the source team primarily tacit or explicit?	The receiving team is asking for explicit knowledge from the source teams. The source teams either immediately know the answer or recognize that they do not know, and do not attempt to reply.
How many functional areas of the organization will be impacted by implementing the knowledge? One team? One division? The whole organization?	The knowledge that the receiving team obtains impacts only that team and that team's success.

DESIGN GUIDELINES FOR EXPERT TRANSFER

Expert Transfer systems probably outnumber any other type of knowledge transfer system. Not only are they relatively easy to establish but they are also immediately and obviously useful. There are, however, design guidelines that allow them to be more effective.

ELECTRONIC FORUMS ARE SEGMENTED BY TOPIC

Electronic forums are typically segmented by topic so that requests go only to those who have the knowledge and the interests to provide a useful answer. Segmentation is important for two reasons. First, it reduces the number of requests received (requests are targeted rather than broadcast). This is critical because if people begin to receive too many requests or requests that are unrelated to their area of expertise, they tend to just delete the messages without taking the time to read them. Second, if the requests are sent only to people who have the same general knowledge as the sender, the requests and responses can be brief—lengthy explanations of what everyone already knows are not needed.

These forums are often tied to networked groups or communities of practice, many of which hold network meetings, offer special training, or send out general announcements related to a topic of interest. So the forums are seldom stand-alone.

ELECTRONIC FORUMS ARE MONITORED AND SUPPORTED

Electronic forums require a considerable amount of support to work well. I have talked with members of many organizations who tell me some version of "Yes, we used to have a system like that, but it just died away. I asked a question a couple of times, but I never got an answer. It finally just got to where nobody ever went in."

Monitoring and support come in several forms:

APPOINTING A PERSON TO THE MONITORING ROLE—One or more persons are appointed to monitor and support each forum. This is often a full-time position rather than an additional responsibility. E&Y calls that person a "knowledge steward." There is a need for both technical monitoring and subject matter monitoring. At Buckman, both a librarian and a sysop have responsibilities, but each may monitor several such forums. Often the subject matter specialist is appointed on a part-time basis. I will reference that person here as a monitor, recognizing that different labels are used in different organizations.

MAKING SURE QUESTIONS ARE ANSWERED—A monitor is responsible for checking to see whether responses have been made to each question, usually within a set time period. If no response is forthcoming, the monitor sends it directly to a source that can provide an answer.

ARCHIVING THE RESPONSES—When responses have stopped coming in, or after a specified period of time, the monitor is responsible for summarizing what was offered, assigning keywords for search, and placing the summary where it can be retrieved by other users. Archiving can substantially reduce the number of requests because the person needing the knowledge can first search the archive and make a request only when the sought-after information is not available. It is clear that if the same knowledge is requested over and over again, people will tend to stop responding and reading as well.

ESTABLISHING GENERAL GUIDELINES—The monitor articulates the agreed-upon guidelines of the group. For example, one of the common mistakes users make is to reply to "all" instead of to an individual when the message is unique to the requester. Monitors can contact responders to explain or reexplain how each type of response works. This kind of support facilitates the smooth functioning of the system.

ATTENDING TO CULTURAL DIFFERENCES—The monitors can alter the format to fit new or changing requirements of the group. In the Buckman Labs example, the monitors set up specific language forums and provided special summaries to different groups. This kind of support requires both resources and an interest in hearing from users about what would best serve their needs.

DIFFERING LEVELS OF PARTICIPATION ARE ENCOURAGED

In most electronic networks only a small percentage of network members respond to the questions that are asked. Buckman Labs estimates between 10 and 20 percent. Although the percentage of people *making* requests is higher, any one individual may put a request out on the forum only once a year or even less frequently.

That the percentages of responders and even of requesters are low is not necessarily an indication that the system is not functioning effectively. In all such systems a large number of people will be passive participants, reading and benefiting from the responses without contributing. Even a small number of contributors can sustain a generalized norm of knowledge sharing in an organization.[2] In the end, the perception of sharing may be as important as the reality, because the idea that people can get help from others via an electronic exchange legitimizes knowledge sharing. And that legitimization may, in fact, translate into other forms of knowledge sharing at the team or system level.

KNOWLEDGE IS PULLED

Electronic forums are a pull system. But they are not a pull system in which users must take the time to search for possible answers in a large database, as many pull systems require (although searching may be necessary when previous responses are archived). The e-forum is a very specific type of pull system in which the requester makes a specific request and the answers are pulled from a targeted community, not from a database. There is no opportunity to get back a thousand hits of which three are useful, as happens in many database pull systems.

BUSINESS DRIVER

Expert Transfer reduces the amount of time it takes teams to resolve nonroutine technical issues that they come across. Buckman claims a reduction in the response time to customers from weeks to days, and since 1987, an increase in the percentage of sales from products that are less than five years old from 14 to 35 percent. BP touts a decrease in the number of helicopter trips to offshore oil platforms that amounted to a savings of $30 million in the first year it implemented its virtual team concept.

BARRIERS AND PROBLEMS

The barriers to Expert Transfer are gradually being lowered, but they do still exist and have to be dealt with.

OUR TECHNOLOGY IS NOT SOPHISTICATED ENOUGH TO CONNECT PEOPLE

Compatible hardware and software is a bare minimum for making Expert Transfer work. Many of the other forms of knowledge transfer do not rely so heavily on technology, but Expert Transfer does. The problems are particularly difficult for multinationals that have units in developing countries.

It is a matter both of software compatibility between units and of having enough computer equipment in the organization. When E&Y began its emphasis on knowledge management, the first thing it did was provide every consultant with a laptop. BP invested heavily in computers and videoconferencing equipment as a first step in its knowledge-sharing effort. That investment has paid off, but the initial investment had to be made.

Organizations use various work-arounds. The World Bank, active as it is in many developing countries, relies heavily on a help line. When someone needs the help of an expert and can't get on-line, the help desk can submit the question or sometimes even directly answer it. But in the end Expert Transfer requires the technology.

Most companies wind up making a choice. Either wait until everyone can get on-line or set up a system for Expert Transfer for those that can get in. Most opt for the latter than rather the former.

OUR PEOPLE AREN'T COMPUTER LITERATE

I can remember when being computer literate was a big issue. You couldn't even boot a computer without a considerable amount of training. But now I wonder if the term "computer literate" hasn't outlived its usefulness. I do think there are still people in organizations who don't want anything to do with computers, but I think this is less of an issue than it has been in the past. The question of whether people on the factory floor or on the rig have the computer equipment available is probably more salient than whether they are computer literate.

That said, there is still probably some need for training. Ford puts its Focal Points through two hours of training. E&Y puts a trainer on the road to go into local offices and show consultants how to use the software. Predictably, those with the lowest skill levels are the most senior people.

SUMMARY

Expert Transfer facilitates the sharing of explicit and often very technical knowledge. It allows a company to make much greater use of its scarce technical expertise. There are two ways, within Expert Transfer, that a team can get an answer to a technical question: (1) the receiving team can broadcast the question to colleagues who are likely to have the answer, or (2) it can use a yellow pages function to identify a specific individual whose expertise listing makes it likely that he or she would have the answer. The "Does anybody know . . . ?" method requires very little time, those responding spending on average only nine minutes and the receivers requiring not much more time to post the question and read the responses. The yellow pages method involves a little more up-front time to locate the right source but has the advantage of ensuring that the request is not overlooked by someone who has the answer. One virtue of Expert Transfer systems is the specificity of the requests and the parsimony of the answers. If the questions asked were more complex, the corresponding answers might also have to be more lengthy,

TABLE 7-1

DESIGN GUIDELINES FOR EXPERT TRANSFER

Definition	A team facing a technical question beyond the scope of its own knowledge seeks the expertise of others in the organization.
Similarity of task and context	The receiving team does a different task from that of the source team, but in a similar context.
Nature of the task	Infrequent and routine
Type of knowledge	Explicit knowledge
Design guidelines	Electronic forums are segmented by topic
	Electronic forums are monitored and supported
	Differing levels of participation are encouraged
	Knowledge is pulled
Example	Technician e-mails the network asking how to increase the brightness on out-of-date monitors. Seven experts provide answers.

requiring time commitments that would surely preclude many people from answering.

Either way, the question is known to the receiving team, so the search is for a source of knowledge. It is an interesting turnaround from Far Transfer, in which the receiving team may not know what question it needs to ask and the search is often for "What have I missed?" That is a difficult question to ask using the "Does anybody know . . . ?" method.

Table 7–1 shows the design guidelines for Expert Transfer. In the next chapter I will look across all five types of knowledge transfer systems for the underlying patterns.

CHAPTER 8

LOOKING ACROSS THE FIVE TYPES OF KNOWLEDGE TRANSFER

CHAPTER BY CHAPTER I HAVE OUTLINED FIVE TYPES OF KNOWL-edge transfer. In table 8–1 I have combined them all in what I hope will be a useful summary. I intend the table to deliver the two fundamental messages of this book: (1) there are many, very different ways to transfer knowledge, and (2) knowledge is transferred most effectively when the transfer process "fits" the knowledge being transferred.

The all-inclusive table provides a brief definition of each type of transfer at the top of each column and an example at the bottom. The core of the table is the design guidelines associated with each type. The guidelines can serve as a checklist for groups that have the responsibility for constructing knowledge transfer systems. But they also serve to point out the need for careful thinking about the design. It matters, for example, whether reports are forwarded in Serial Transfer; the number of items pushed to sites makes a difference in Near Transfer. That

143

TABLE 8-1

FIVE TYPES OF KNOWLEDGE TRANSFER

	SERIAL TRANSFER	NEAR TRANSFER	FAR TRANSFER	STRATEGIC TRANSFER	EXPERT TRANSFER
Definition	The knowledge a team has gained from doing its task in one setting is transferred to the next time that team does the task in a different setting.	Explicit knowledge a team has gained from doing a frequent and repeated task is reused by other teams doing very similar work.	Tacit knowledge a team has gained from doing a nonroutine task is made available to other teams doing similar work in another part of the organization.	The collective knowledge of the organization is needed to accomplish a strategic task that occurs infrequently but is critical to the whole organization.	A team facing a technical question beyond the scope of its own knowledge seeks the expertise of others in the organization.
Similarity of task and context	The receiving team (which is also the source team) does a similar task in a new context.	The receiving team does a task similar to that of the source team and in a similar context.	The receiving team does a task similar to that of the source team but in a different context.	The receiving team does a task that impacts the whole organization in a context different from that of the source team.	The receiving team does a different task from that of the source team, but in a similar context.
Nature of the task	Frequent and nonroutine	Frequent and routine	Frequent and nonroutine	Infrequent and nonroutine	Infrequent and routine
Type of knowledge	Tacit and explicit	Explicit	Tacit	Tacit and explicit	Explicit
Design guidelines	Meetings are held regularly	Knowledge is disseminated electronically	Exchange is reciprocal	Knowledge needed is identified by senior-level managers	Electronic forums are segmented by topic

Design guidelines (continued)	Meetings are brief	Electronic dissemination is supplemented by personal interaction	Source team knowledge is translated	Knowledge specialists collect and interpret the knowledge	Electronic forums are monitored and supported
	Everyone involved in the action participates in the meeting	Users specify the content and format	People carry the knowledge across the organization	Collection occurs in real time rather than retrospectively	Differing levels of participation are encouraged
	There are no recriminations	Knowledge is pushed	Process is given a recognizable name	Focus is on the end user	Knowledge is pulled
	Reports are not forwarded	A limited number of items are pushed		Multiple voices are synthesized	
	Meetings are facilitated locally	There is compliance with choice			
		Usage and business goals are monitored			
		Brief descriptions are adequate			
		The database is targeted			
Example	A power generator replacement team replaces a generator in a chemical plant. The team uses that knowledge when replacing a generator in a refinery.	A team in an Atlanta auto plant figures out how to install brakes in ten seconds. A team in Chicago uses that knowledge to reduce its time by fifteen seconds.	Peers travel to assist a team dealing with a unique oil exploration site. The collaboration provides new approaches.	A company acquires ABC; six months later another team in a different location uses what was learned with ABC to acquire DFG.	Technician e-mails the network asking how to increase the brightness on out-of-date monitors. Seven experts provide answers.

is not to say that every guideline is required for each type. But if a guideline is omitted it needs to be with an understanding of the purpose it serves and the consequences of excepting it.

Table 8–1 also details the criteria for choosing one type of transfer over another. I provided a rationale for each criterion in chapter 2 and offered a set of questions that help to determine whether each criterion applies to a specific situation. In figure 8–1 I offer a simplified decision tree based on the same criteria. The questions asked in the decision tree in order are:

Will the same team be using what has been learned?

Is the knowledge tacit?

Does the knowledge impact the whole organization?

Is the task routine and frequent?

USING MULTIPLE TYPES OF TRANSFER SYSTEMS

Organizations need to transfer many different kinds of knowledge for many different purposes. Many of the organizations I have written about have developed multiple ways to transfer knowledge. The U.S. Army, for example, makes use of both AARs (Serial Transfer) and collectors in the field (Strategic Transfer). British Petroleum uses AARs (Serial Transfer), Knowledge Assets (Strategic Transfer), Connect (Expert Transfer), Peer Assist (Far Transfer), and Intranet discussion groups among network members (Expert Transfer). These fit into BP's model of learning before, learning during, and learning after, which has the advantage of being easy to remember and serves to remind teams that knowledge is involved in *every* part of their work.

Other organizations, however, find a model that successfully transfers one kind of knowledge and then seem to get stuck in that category. For example, Ford has, in some ways, been a victim of its own success with Best Practice Replication (Near Transfer). In three and a half years BPR has saved Ford $370 million, which makes it difficult to not view BPR as "the" answer. But this success may have prevented Ford from developing processes that could transfer different kinds of knowledge, particularly complex knowledge, that might be of considerable strategic help.

FIGURE 8-1

DECISION TREE FOR SELECTING TYPE OF TRANSFER

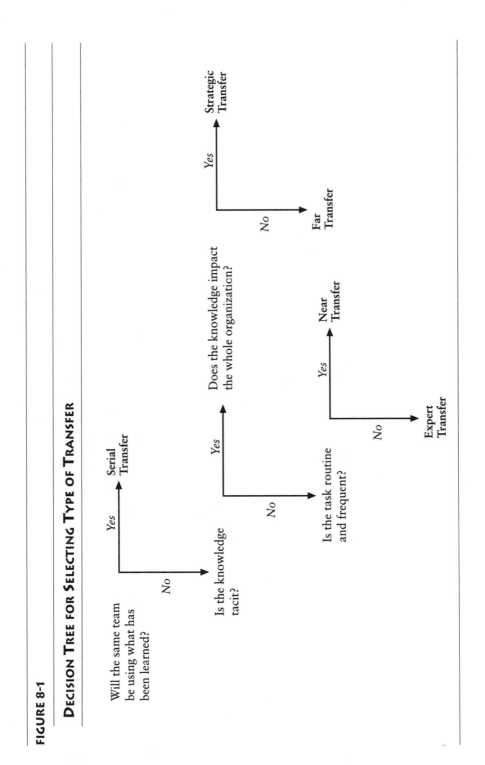

To some extent that has been true of E&Y as well. Its concentration has been on sharing "client-facing" knowledge in the form of "naturally occurring work products." It has supported the Knowledge Web (Near Transfer) with network meetings and hard-tagged consultants (Far Transfer), but there is still a great deal of knowledge that E&Y consulting teams could construct through Serial Transfer or Strategic Transfer.

Likewise, Buckman Labs has built a strong competence in Expert Transfer and has been widely acclaimed for its excellence in the transfer of technical knowledge between individuals, but it has put less focus on transferring other kinds of knowledge.

It is critical to develop multiple approaches for transfer rather than relying on a single approach, regardless of how successful that approach is. Every organization has a range of knowledge, tacit and explicit, routine and nonroutine, strategic and team-specific, that makes it competitive. Organizations need ways to transfer knowledge in all five of the categories I have outlined in this book. It is not a matter of choosing the best *one* to implement in an organization. Rather the task is to identify the kinds of knowledge that need to be transferred and to design processes that will successfully transfer each type of knowledge. The identification and the design are evolving tasks rather than one-time selections.

CHANGING HOW WE THINK ABOUT KNOWLEDGE

The preceding five chapters have each looked at one type of transfer and shown the way it is different from the other types in terms of the knowledge, the task, and the recipient it supports. Now I want to look across all five types of knowledge transfer to note patterns in how organizations are thinking about knowledge. Three major shifts are discernible across all five types of transfer.

- The first is a shift from thinking of experts as the primary source of knowledge to thinking that everyone engaged in work tasks has knowledge someone else could use to advantage.

- The second is a shift from thinking of knowledge as residing with individuals to thinking of knowledge as embedded in a group or community.

- The third is a shift from thinking of knowledge as a stable commodity to thinking of knowledge as dynamic and ever changing.

We are in the midst of these changes, so sometimes organizations act out of the newer perceptions and sometimes out of their former perceptions. And sometimes they even invent a process to transfer knowledge based on the newer perceptions, but then implement it in a manner based on the older perceptions.

I call these changes "shifts," but perhaps the term is not really accurate because it implies leaving something old behind and taking up something new. It may be more accurate to say that our understanding of knowledge in organizational settings is becoming broader, more comprehensive. I will address each of the three shifts in turn, although, in the end, they all intersect each other.

FROM EXPERT TO DISTRIBUTED

The most profound change I have observed is a shift away from the idea that knowledge is found only in a *select group of experts* or "best" practitioners and toward the idea that useful knowledge is *distributed* throughout the whole of an organization.

In the past, if I had asked top managers in an organization where the organization's critical knowledge was, they would probably have ticked off a list of employees they considered Subject Matter Experts (SMEs) in the areas of competitive importance to the organization. In an oil company that might be the people who knew the most about topics like horizontal drilling and refinery maintenance; in manufacturing it might be people who knew the most about product and process flow.

If the organization was facing a really tough problem in one of those areas, management might put together a task force of the experts from around the company to come up with a solution.

FIGURE 8-2

THE EXPERT MODEL: KNOWLEDGE IS TRANSFERRED FROM A FEW DESIGNATED EXPERTS

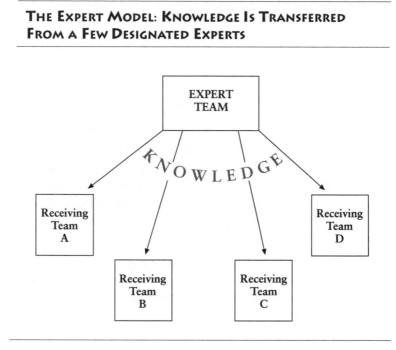

Once the task force had completed its work, management would send the identified solution out to be implemented by those who were less "in the know." The flow of knowledge would look something like figure 8–2. It would move from the experts to those who were less expert. I will label this way of thinking about who has knowledge the "expert model."

I could in fact use the same model to demonstrate knowledge moving from a manager to subordinates or from a professor to students. In each situation there is an individual or a group that carries the organization's approbation and others that are expected to emulate the expert group.

That familiar view of knowledge has begun to evolve into a very different idea about who has useful knowledge: the view of knowledge as widely distributed across organizational members rather than residing in a small number of experts. Most of the transfer practices described in this book did not start by trying to identify who was doing some critical practice "the best." They

FIGURE 8-3

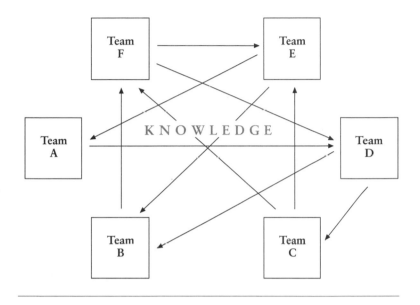

THE DISTRIBUTED MODEL:
KNOWLEDGE IS TRANSFERRED AMONG TEAMS

started from the assumption that nearly every team was doing something that others in the organization could make use of, and likewise could use what others knew. These knowledge transfer systems are designed to facilitate a give-and-take among peers. I will label this newer way of thinking about who in the organization has important knowledge the "distributed model," to indicate that knowledge is located in a multitude of diverse people and places across the organization.

I have represented the distributed view of organizational knowledge in figure 8–3. If we assume that Team A, B, C, D, E, and F are all teams within an organization, we see that A's knowledge is shared with D; likewise D has some knowledge that B and C make use of, and so on. In this figure the knowledge flows from multiple sources to multiple receivers. There is no hint that Team A is more expert or somehow smarter than Team B, C, D, E, or F. Knowledge transfer goes on among "like people" rather than flowing from the "best" to the "less able." This is a reciprocal model in which all contribute and all receive.

Many examples of the distributed model have appeared in this book. For example, Ford's Best Practice Replication System facilitates the transfer of knowledge among Ford's Vehicle Operations plants around the world. And although Ford calls this system Best Practice Replication, the system is clearly not about a plant being "best." Rather, the way the system is designed is an acknowledgment that each Vehicle Operations plant has something to offer the other plants. In fact, a central element of the system is the summary report of all thirty-seven plants that shows how many practices each plant has contributed and how many each has adopted. If a regional manager notices that a particular plant in his region has contributed few new practices, he puts pressure on that plant to increase its submissions because it is assumed that there *are* practices that are occurring in that plant that would be of use to others.

A very different example of the distributed model that I talked about is British Petroleum's Peer Assist. The assisters are not corporate staff, nor are they in any hierarchical or reporting relationship to those who are asking for assistance; rather, they are peers who in the coming months are likely to be asking others to give them the same kind of assistance. The assisters do not arrive with a dog and pony show, nor do they come to brag about what they have already accomplished; the focus of the meeting is rather on the specific objectives that the team making the request has laid out. When I am giving presentations about the distributed model, I often use Peer Assist as an example. Sometimes participants mention Peer Review as a similar process in their own organizations. And although I recognize that a Peer Review process shares characteristics with Peer Assist, it seems to me to be more closely related to the expert model. That is, a Peer Review team offers useful advice, but it is offered from a position of evaluation. The flow of knowledge is from those who have been designated as official representatives to those who are being judged. The striking difference with Peer Assist is that the peers who come to assist learn as much as those being assisted—there is a reciprocal exchange. The difference between a Peer Review and a Peer Assist, as subtle as it may be, is at the heart of the changing perception about who in the organization has credible knowledge.

A third example is Lockheed Martin's LM21 Best Practices. The benchmarking Lockheed Martin did at the front end of its transfer process provided ample evidence that knowledge was widely distributed across its many heritage companies. The design it has used to make knowledge sharing happen, Transfer Teams, manifests that understanding by building reciprocity in on several levels; the source team members provide their knowledge and are themselves learning from the receiving team members; the source teams learn from each other since there are two units serving in the source role on each team; and the source teams become receiving teams for other practices.

In each of these examples of knowledge transfer, as well as others in the book, an extensive amount of activity related to knowledge is taking place in the organization. Much of the organizational knowledge produced during this heightened activity would have been lost, or more likely never developed, if these systems had been designed by engineers who were constrained by the assumptions of the expert model. When transfer systems are based on that model, the knowledge activity is limited to a one-way dissemination in which the intent is to identify the best ideas and then disseminate them—a useful but much less vigorous knowledge exchange.

The expert model is, however, still very present in organizations even while the distributed model is growing alongside it. In fact, during my study I saw many knowledge transfer systems that were based on the assumptions of the expert model, some of which were successful and others whose success was more limited. Even in those that were successful I noted that an unintended consequence of the expert model was to trigger the ubiquitous Not Invented Here syndrome. That syndrome was less evident in transfer systems based on the distributed model, perhaps because teams were more willing to accept what others created when they observed that those teams were making use of their ideas as well.

The distributed model, then, provides considerable advantage to an organization that is designing a knowledge transfer system by facilitating a more dynamic exchange and by reducing resistance to reuse. Even so, the transition is not easily made from expert to distributed model. Organizations have had years of experience in creating systems to transfer expert knowledge (e.g., training classes, journals, books, consultant contracts, and so on). Thus the assumptions of the expert model can influence decisions without managers even being aware that those assumptions are in place.

In the distributed model, organizational members who have firsthand experience with the work or task are seen as viable sources of both existing and new knowledge. A growing recognition is that organizational members in the act of doing their jobs are capable of inventing effective processes. "Some competencies may be on the factory floor, some in the R & D labs, some in the executive suites. The key to organizational knowledge is to weave it all together. Successful organizational synthesis of knowledge requires discovering knowledge as and where it emerges in practice. That can't be done if when and where to look are predetermined *ex ante*."[1]

In my zeal to explain this interesting shift in the view of where useful knowledge is located within organizations, I don't want to overstate my case. I am not suggesting that *any* knowledge that *any* team or individual has developed is automatically valid or indeed worth replicating. Many teams and individuals learn something through their experience that is, in fact, not helpful to the organization. There is, however, an interesting built-in safeguard that comes with the idea of distributed knowledge. Because no official is declaring the knowledge that is moving around the organization as the "best" or the "answer," decisions about reusing the knowledge are left in the hands of the recipients. The criterion for choosing what knowledge to incorporate becomes the usefulness of the knowledge to a specific situation—the fit.

That is a different criterion than teams would have used in the past. In the expert model it is the organization that legitimizes knowledge by labeling it as a "best practice" or as the "GE way." The knowledge is considered valid because the organization's leadership, the academic community, or scientific study stands behind it. We would all recognize the fallibility of that thinking, yet we might all use it, when needed, to bolster our argument because we recognize its currency.

In the distributed model it is not possible to rely on authority for assurance of validity, because what the knowledge teams receive from others does not pass through or arise from "authoritative" sources. Rather, the knowledge arises from the experience of others who are engaged in real work; "ground truth" is increasingly being seen as valid.

When I asked the leader of BP's Venezuela restructuring team if he regarded what the Colombia team had done as "best practice," he acknowledged that the Venezuela team had had some discussion about why it was willing to make use of what it found in the Knowledge Asset.

> We asked ourselves, "Why are we basing this on Colombia? Did they do it particularly well?" And our answer was they have gone through two restructurings so they must have learned lessons from the first one that they used in the second. Hopefully we could build on those lessons. We saw it as fertile learning ground because they had a chance to iterate and learn from the first time. The reason we were interested was because they did it once and then had to do it again—so they must have learned from it. By going through it and perhaps more importantly by talking with Nick [a member of BP's central knowledge management group] about it, they had some structure around ordering it, understanding it, communicating it. They [Colombia] are not saying "We did it best." But they were hoping others would build on it and communicate what they have done.

This thoughtful response reveals that the Venezuela team was not viewing what was in the Knowledge Asset as "definitive practice" or the "way to do it," but the team did respect that experience brings with it knowledge and thus assumed that the Colombia team had learned something that Venezuela might be able to use. The measure the Venezuela team used for acceptance of this knowledge was whether it "fit" the Venezuela situation. The team members arrived at conclusions about fit by talking through what they had learned from Colombia and how it might, or might not, work for them. Colombia was a source of ideas and perspective for Venezuela, not a definitive answer.

KNOWLEDGE AS A GROUP PHENOMENON

The second major shift that is occurring in how organizations think about knowledge is the shift from thinking of it as an individual phenomenon to thinking of it as a group or community phenomenon. Our strong bias toward thinking of knowledge as an individual phenomenon is, in large part, a result of our lengthy school experience. In school we were encouraged to "do our own work," to study in a quiet place like a library where we would not be disturbed by others, and not to cheat on tests, meaning that we were not to get help from others. These norms, which are very enduring for us, tell us that learning is something that we do on our own—an independent activity. These ideas have influenced not only how we think about learning and knowledge in school but also how we think about knowledge in the broader organizational context as well.

Yet, despite the power of these past messages, organizational members are beginning to think of knowledge as being constructed within a community or group. One of the new terms that has come into our organizational vocabulary, "communities of practice," gives us the beginnings of a language to talk about this new way of thinking about knowledge. The term originated with Jean Lave and Etienne Wenger's book *Situated Learning* and was brought to even greater clarity in Wenger's book *Communities of Practice*.[2] Wenger believes that knowledge is developed as we actively participate in the practices of a social community. That community may be a work team, a church group, a family group, or a soccer team.

All of us belong to many such communities, and our learning and knowledge within each are central to our sense of belonging to that community. Our knowledge of how to be a parent, a team player, or an effective systems analyst is a part of our identity and sense of competence. Knowledge is not in addition to such roles, it is in service of them. Wenger, then, is suggesting that we cannot divorce knowledge from participating in the community in which that knowledge is exercised.

In the acknowledgment section of *Communities of Practice*, Wenger tells this story: "A while ago, I asked my colleague Jean Lave in exactly which publication she had first introduced the term community of practice. We had used the term in a book we wrote together, but I wanted to give her proper credit for originating it. To my surprise, she replied: 'I thought you were the one who came up with it.' "[3]

That conversation would be a familiar one to many of us who have been a part of a group or team in which knowledge and ideas seemed to grow and change as they flitted from person to person, until it was no longer possible to say who originated a particular idea. Many innovative ideas could not have been created by a single individual; it took the diversity of minds and the synergy of ideas to reach the prized goal. Yet often organizations, by their reward policies or individualized performance goals, induce employees to report ideas as their own— in fact, to think of knowledge as an individual phenomenon.

Chaparral Steel, which has made a name for itself as a learning organization, has operationalized the idea that knowledge is a social phenomenon. At Chaparral they do not single out individuals for praise. Chaparral believes that if individuals are singled out they will begin to protect good ideas rather than share them. At Chaparral it is understood that ideas go through a gestation period where lots of people figure out how to make the idea work. In fact, Chaparral employees are often unable to identify the source of a production innovation. Neither are employees singled out for blame; there is an absence of punitive actions following failures. As Wenger notes in relating his story of the origin of the term "communities of practice," "Dissecting a creation to assign individual credit can easily become counterproductive."

The way that the U.S. Army's CALL system creates knowledge is an example of a community constructing knowledge. The collectors draw on their extensive networks to plan the questions to ask in the field. They send what they are collecting back to CALL, where colleagues continue the analysis and reframe questions for the collectors to ask. Even the analysts at

CALL send their preliminary synthesis to colleagues for review and comment. At CALL it is a community that jointly constructs the knowledge.

AARs are another example of the shift from viewing knowledge as individual to thinking of knowledge as a group phenomenon. It is not difficult to imagine that in times past, at the end of a military action, the general would sit by himself in his tent carefully thinking through what had worked well and what had gone poorly during the action, and then would call his sergeant in to give the orders about how to improve the next action on the basis of his very competent analysis. That is a very heroic, and for that reason very attractive, picture. We like to think of leaders as very wise, even all knowing.

By contrast, the assumption behind AARs is that in order to understand the action that has just happened everybody that was involved needs to think together about it. And in order to construct knowledge about what to do next, everybody is going to have to think together. Thinking about jointly constructing knowledge in this way has a very different meaning from the old adage about involving everyone so they won't resist the proposed change. AARs are not about seeking the compliance of team members but about making use of their knowledge-constructing ability—a very different proposition altogether.

Peer Assist is also about the joint construction of knowledge. It is based on the underlying assumption that others, with a fresh perspective born out of a different set of related experiences, can help a team think about an important issue it is facing.

I want to note, however, that the construction of knowledge is different from decision making. The team that calls for the assist still has the responsibility to decide what it will do, and the general still makes the decision after the AAR. The joint construction of knowledge *informs* the decision but does not *make* the decision.

KNOWLEDGE AS DYNAMIC

The third shift that is occurring in how we think about knowledge is from thinking of it as something that is stable to thinking of it as something that is changeable and changing. In chapter 1, I talked about the warehouse image that so easily comes to mind when we hear about the need to "collect, store, and disseminate knowledge." The warehouse metaphor references knowledge as a stable commodity that can be stored, almost like a piece of furniture, and then taken out whenever it is needed.

The dynamic view of knowledge regards it as constantly changing and altering even in its use and reuse. When assisters fly home from a Peer Assist they take with them different knowledge than the knowledge they came with. Learning historians do not just report what they learned through a team's action; the questions they have asked and the insights they have offered alter the way the experience is understood by all those who have been involved in it. The dynamic view conceives of knowledge as a temporary explanation that we can use to guide our actions—a necessary temporary explanation, but temporary nonetheless. David Bohm notes: "We have to have enough faith in our worldview to work from it, but not that much faith that we think it's the final answer."[4]

If the warehouse is a metaphor for the stable view of knowledge, then a metaphor for the dynamic view of knowledge may be *water flowing across*; the water represents knowledge that is continually in motion across the organization, always in play. The warehouse image has about it a feeling of control—the certainty of being able to grasp the knowledge of the organization and maybe even keep it from walking out the door. The flowing water image seems less controllable but also more powerful—after all, there is little that can stand in the way of flowing water.

The U.S. Army's CALL system provides an example of the flow of knowledge in an organization. The knowledge moves from collectors, to CALL analysts, to the functional home unit of the collectors, to the analysts' colleagues in the field, to training, and so on. This knowledge is constantly in motion, being reshaped and reconfigured as it moves around the organization.

If the designers of transfer systems thought of knowledge as dynamic, they might design conduits to enhance its flow rather than warehouses for its storage. Their planning might be about how to maximize the movement of knowledge across the organization. Their focus might be on creating a system in which every time knowledge moves from team to team new ideas get added to it to make it more effective.

Images are powerful thinking tools. How we imagine knowledge in an organization—whether as moving in one direction or distributed, whether as stored in a warehouse or flowing across an organization, whether as held in one person's mind or as abiding in a collective—impacts how knowledge transfer systems are designed. "Our design is hostage to our understanding, perspectives and theories."[5]

CHAPTER 9

BUILDING AN INTEGRATED SYSTEM FOR KNOWLEDGE TRANSFER

ALL OF THE SUCCESSFUL TRANSFER SYSTEMS I HAVE DESCRIBED in this book are integrated systems. The actual carrier of the knowledge, whether that is e-mail, a group of peers traveling to a site, or a database, is only one element in a much larger system that makes the transfer effective. For example, a listing of the elements of Ford's Best Practice Replication would include:

1. the database that distributes the best practices,

2. the designated Focal Points in each plant who receive the items and in turn submit items,

3. a limited number of items and a requirement to respond to them,

4. plant management meetings at which decisions are made about adoption of the ideas,

5. the response and tracking system that produces and distributes reports of replication activity,

6. regional management meetings where the tracking reports are reviewed,

7. frequent face-to-face meetings of production engineers at various plants across Ford,

8. each plant's productivity requirement, which drives the continual search for new ideas to reduce costs, and

9. a small central staff of half a dozen people who maintain the system and market it internally to other parts of Ford.

Not only are there many elements, but each element works to reinforce and support the others. What I consistently hear at the many knowledge management conferences I attend is that companies should not ignore the human or cultural side of knowledge sharing. I would not disagree with that idea, but I think dichotomizing knowledge sharing into technological and cultural components is misleading. Some of the components listed above could be put in one category or the other, but many could not. On which side would Ford's 5 percent task fall? Or the regional management meetings? Or the requirement to respond? And some of the transfer systems I have discussed, such as AARs, have no technological component at all. The issue is not about adding human components to a technological system but how to build an integrated system in which each element is integrated with the other elements to make the whole work as a system. Among the elements that need to be integrated, the following six are of primary importance:

THE RELATIONSHIP BETWEEN THE KNOWLEDGE TO BE TRANSFERRED AND THE LARGER GOALS OF THE UNIT OR ORGANIZATION. The management group that establishes the larger goals must construct this relationship. Constructing it involves more than just naming it or pointing it out; it requires ferreting out the actual links between certain kinds of knowledge and organizational goals. If there is no relationship between some of the organization's goals and its knowledge, or the link is so slight as to be intangible, these are not the goals on which to build a knowledge transfer system. The relationship between specific knowledge and specific goals also needs to be readily apparent to those who are expected to use the system.

This element speaks to the concept of "compliance with choice" that I talked about in chapter 4. The goals are the compliance part of the equation. As an example, the items that come across Ford's BPR are directly related to the 5 percent productivity improvement each plant is required to make. Knowledge is the "choice" part of the equation.

THE SPECIFIC POPULATION THE SYSTEM TARGETS. To be effective a transfer system needs to be designed for a specific population that has a specific knowledge need. For example, Chevron's Project Resources targets project managers of capital-intensive projects. Likewise E&Y's PowerPacks are designed for consultants within a specific industry segment. An organization may need many transfer systems for many unique populations. Transfer systems are less useful and less effective when they are designed for just "anyone" in the organization.

THE SPECIFIC BENEFIT THE TARGET POPULATION RECEIVES FROM PARTICIPATING. The way the target population benefits from participating needs to be direct and obvious to it. Unless the benefit is direct, that is, the knowledge is needed in order to accomplish the target's work task, the transfer is less effective. For example, the benefit to a team that responds to the alerts sent through TI's Alert Notification System is evident to those who then make changes to avoid a potential disaster. Likewise, for teams that call a Peer Assist to get ideas that help them make a better decision, the reasoning is unambiguous. There is nothing wrong with secondary benefits, like cash awards or recognition; they just cannot substitute for direct benefits.

HOW THE SYSTEM IS MONITORED. By monitoring I don't mean just counting the number of hits on the database or the number of times a group meets. I mean who is paying attention; who notices and cares what is going on. Bob Buckman's attention to his company's Techforums makes a difference. Lockheed Martin's LM21 is monitored by a steering committee that reports directly to the CEO. If knowledge sharing is tied to organizational or unit goals in a clear and direct way, then the organization will track both the transfer activity and the goal.

WHO HAS SPECIFIC RESPONSIBILITIES FOR KNOWLEDGE TRANSFER. In most organizations people are overloaded with tasks; they have only limited time that they can devote to knowledge transfer. So saying that "everybody" needs to contribute often means that "nobody" feels particularly responsible. Organizations need designated resources, people with specific skills or who have had additional training, to make all the parts of a knowledge transfer system work. For example, members of the Central Management Team are the designated collectors of the learning that goes into BP's Knowledge Asset. The Focal Points at Ford are the designated receivers and are responsible for input.

THE CONTROL OF THE SYSTEM. This element is about how the rules are made about what content is appropriate. It is a question of what corporate "owns" and what the users "own." The concept of "compliance with choice" would suggest that corporate owns the compliance part of the formula and that the choice of what knowledge is needed and what format it is in belongs to the users. For example, Ford production engineers define the parameters for the best practices that are entered into the system, such as requiring that any practice offered needs to already be up and running in a plant, or that video is necessary as well as print. At BP the team that calls a Peer Assist specifies the objectives for the meeting.

The integration of these six elements, and perhaps others, has to be carefully and thoughtfully designed from the beginning so that the parts do not contradict or work against each other in ways that defeat the intent of the system. For this reason the integrated design needs to be rooted in a framework into which the elements fit. An example of a framework is "making connections between people," which has guided the design of BP's knowledge transfer efforts. The principle of "ground truth" serves as a framework for the U.S. Army's CALL. Throughout the book I have sketched a number of such frameworks. One of the most powerful is the idea of distributed knowledge, which I described in the last chapter. In that chapter I also talked about knowledge as a group phenomenon and knowledge as dynamic rather than stable. These ideas, individually or together, can provide a framework that integrates the elements of a system in a consistent and reinforcing way.

Getting Started

One of the most difficult problems in this very complex business of knowledge transfer is how and where to start. I offer here a series of steps focused on that issue. The steps place the selection of the type of transfer used into a larger framework and allow me to summarize many of the concepts of the book.

Select a Unit That Has Interest in knowledge Sharing

Some companies are fortunate to have a CEO who supports the need for knowledge transfer and can articulate that need for the organization. John Browne at BP has played that role, as has Bob Buckman of Buckman Labs. But many of the successful efforts I have seen have started in a single division, as Ford's BPR did in Vehicle Operations and Chevron's Capital Project Resources.

In fact, since the most effective knowledge transfer systems target a specific organizational goal and a specific audience, starting in a unit or division has considerable advantage. When Ford's BPR system proved itself in Vehicle Operations it then spread across other Ford divisions, including Body, Stamping, Quality, Finishing, HR, and Central Engineering.

Establish a Steering Committee

An enormous amount of strategic thinking is required to create a successful knowledge transfer system. This is not the nitty-gritty work of running the system but the policy work of establishing a framework, of identifying the critical knowledge the unit needs, of building the connection between a targeted organizational goal and specific knowledge, and of procuring the necessary resources. A steering committee, representative of the whole unit or division, is needed to do this strategic work. The committee needs to be made up of people who are at a high enough level in the organization to make policy decisions about these issues that will stick.

It is important that this not be a committee chaired by someone from the technology or Information Systems (IS) group. Regardless of the reality, if IS is prominent, the perception will be that IS owns the effort and that may well work against the kind of systematic approach offered in this book. It would be difficult, for instance, for IS to lead an effort that includes processes like AAR, Peer Assist, or even Strategic Transfer. IS needs to be represented on the committee but not lead it. The role of IS is to provide the technology pieces after an integrated system has been developed.

The steering committee itself may need some education and preparation for its task. It may want to make site visits to other organizations, read the growing literature on knowledge management, and sponsor an assessment of the current state of the organization's knowledge activities.

CONDUCT A KNOWLEDGE ASSESSMENT

A knowledge assessment is a careful and systematic examination of an organization to identify the following elements:

- What knowledge already exists in the organization that could be usefully leveraged

- What knowledge teams need in order to improve their performance

- What critical processes have the most variance across parts of the organization, making sharing valuable

- What knowledge sharing efforts already exist that could be built on

- What knowledge provides the highest leverage for cost savings

- Which teams are most ready to share and receive knowledge

- What policies or practices in the organization facilitate and constrain knowledge sharing

- Who the stakeholders are and what their interests are

- How the organization's knowledge capability compares to that of other organizations

It is useful to build a team of internal and external members to conduct a knowledge assessment. The external members are able to identify assumptions and opportunities related to knowledge that internal members may not notice; the internal members provide the much-needed context and are a way to retain in-house what is learned from the assessment.

The completed assessment provides the steering committee the information necessary to create a business case that includes lost opportunity costs, potential dollar savings through knowledge transfer, and the costs involved in creating and maintaining a knowledge transfer system.

ESTABLISH THE FRAMEWORK FOR KNOWLEDGE TRANSFER

One of the most important tasks of the steering committee is to think through and then articulate the framework the organization or unit will use for knowledge transfer. In chapter 8, I suggested a number of such frameworks that are consistent with what I have learned from studying successful organizations. However, a framework needs to be stated in the language of the company rather than in my language. It needs to fit the organization and to make intuitive sense both to the steering committee and to those who will make use of it.

It is hard to overemphasize the need for a framework that will guide the policies and implementation of knowledge transfer. Without such a framework, well-intentioned people can establish rules and put processes into place that prevent the system from succeeding. The all too familiar assumptions about such things as expert models and individual knowledge can too easily impact critical decisions.

IDENTIFY AN ORGANIZATIONAL GOAL AND CORRESPONDING KNOWLEDGE COMPONENT

The steering committee is responsible for building the connection between an organizational or unit goal and the specific knowledge that will impact that goal. The knowledge assessment can provide data about where knowledge opportunities exist, but only the steering committee can actually establish the necessary link between the knowledge and the goal.

This task requires an in-depth understanding of where the organization is heading and what goals are of critical importance for its future. Building the relationship between the organizational goal and specific knowledge components is a way to tailor the knowledge transfer process for the organization or unit. It is not effective simply to replicate what another organization has done. Rather, the organizations I have written about in this book and those a steering committee might visit represent a kind of Strategic Transfer. It is possible to understand what has worked elsewhere, why it has worked, and what the reasoning was in the choices that were made, and to use that knowledge to inform the design of a unique transfer for the organization.

In that same regard, if the knowledge transfer effort in an organization is begun at the unit or division level, it would be important for other units to be able to learn from how the steering committee in that unit has done its work. That is, the steering committee and its activities would become the subject of Strategic Transfer. That would require a knowledge specialist who can observe, interview, and document the process in a way that would make it useful for other units.

IDENTIFY THE APPROPRIATE TRANSFER PROCESS FOR EACH TYPE OF KNOWLEDGE

Once high-leverage knowledge has been identified, the committee needs to select the appropriate transfer process for that type of knowledge. A number of different kinds of knowledge may be identified, each of which will require a different transfer process. The identification of the most effective transfer systems involves asking such questions as:

Who is the intended receiver of the knowledge in terms of similarity of task and context?

How routine and frequent is the task?

Is the knowledge tacit or explicit?

The answers to those questions determine whether the knowledge would be most effectively transferred through:

SERIAL TRANSFER—the knowledge a team has learned from doing its task that can be transferred to the next time that team does the task in a different setting.

NEAR TRANSFER—the explicit knowledge a team has gained from doing a frequent and repeated task that the organization would like to replicate in other teams that are doing very similar work.

FAR TRANSFER—the tacit knowledge a team has gained from doing a nonroutine task that the organization would like to make available to other teams that are doing similar work in another part of the organization.

STRATEGIC TRANSFER—the collective knowledge of the organization needed to accomplish a strategic task that occurs infrequently but is of critical importance to the whole organization.

EXPERT TRANSFER—the technical knowledge a team needs that is beyond the scope of its own knowledge but can be found in the special expertise of others in the organization.

The guidelines for designing each of the five types of transfer process ensure that the system is effective.

LOCATE CURRENT INFORMAL SYSTEMS THAT CAN BE ENHANCED

All organizations have ways in which knowledge currently gets shared. Members send off a package of blueprints to a colleague, call a buddy who has faced this same computer glitch, drop by an unusual construction site to see how the work is progressing, or observe a surgical team in action. It is possible to build on these informal systems, using the design guidelines, rather than starting from ground zero. Often a few people at the center of a loose network to whom others turn to get their questions answered can form a nucleus to understand what others are asking for and how it is of assistance to them.

The production engineers in Ford Vehicle Operations plants had devised a paper method of exchanging practices long before their electronic database was developed. When the electronic database was created, it was designed to provide the same type of knowledge the production engineers had been sharing in the paper format and was structured in a way they felt to be most useful. Likewise, before knowledge management efforts at E&Y were in place, it was not uncommon for the leader of a consulting team to pick up the phone to ask a colleague for a copy of his or her workplan or PowerPoint presentation with the hope of making use of parts of it for a similar consulting project. The KnowledgeWeb formalized such informal exchanges and expanded the group of colleagues from whom "naturally occurring work products" could be obtained.

IDENTIFY RESOURCES

Buckman Labs spends $7,500 per person, or 3.5 to 4.5 percent of revenue, on its knowledge efforts. CEO Bob Buckman says plainly, "If you are not prepared to invest at this rate or higher, then you will not get the benefits I described."[1] Those benefits include a stark reduction in response time to customers and an 11 percent increase in the percentage of sales from new products.

E&Y spends 6 percent of its revenue on knowledge management. It also acknowledges an 80 percent reduction in the time it takes teams to prepare a proposal for new business. I have noted throughout the book other results figures that knowledge transfer systems have produced.

Obviously, costs vary depending on the type of system implemented, but all of the knowledge transfer systems have costs associated with them. The question is whether the anticipated gain is worth the costs, and that is a question that a knowledge assessment can help address.

The task for the steering committee is to assess the potential gain and to identify the costs, including personnel needed to collect knowledge or monitor systems, equipment costs, travel costs to move tacit knowledge, the cost of benchmarking and site visits, and consulting costs. Identifying resources also includes decisions about who will play what knowledge roles and whether those roles are made a part of current responsibilities or personnel are added to fill the roles.

DEVELOP AN INTEGRATED SYSTEM FOR KNOWLEDGE TRANSFER

The type of transfer system, the current informal efforts, and the organizational goals all need to be combined to create an integrated system. Each element has to support and reinforce the other elements and all must represent the framework the committee has established. The initial knowledge effort in an organization does not need to start large, but it does need to start as an integrated system.

SUMMARY

The organizations that have allowed me to tell their stories in this book, Bechtel, British Petroleum, Buckman Labs, Chevron, Ernst & Young, Ford, Lockheed Martin, Tandem, Texas Instruments, and the U.S. Army, illustrate how incredibly powerful common knowledge can be for increasing organizational effectiveness. These organizations have achieved enormous dollar savings and productivity increases by finding ways to transfer common knowledge across time and space. I have intentionally drawn my examples from organizations that have been successful because I wanted to understand *why* the processes work when they do. What I discovered is that these organizations know a great deal about *how* their transfer processes work but much less about *why*. And lacking that understanding, the most they can do to pass along their own knowledge at conferences or through journal articles is to encourage others to "do what we did." That they cannot fully articulate the why of knowledge transfer is not surprising because there has been very little systematic study of knowledge transfer in organizations. Organizations, like the ones I have written about in this book, that are on the leading edge of knowledge transfer have been learning on their own, primarily through trial and error.

My goal in writing this book was to begin a systematic look at why transfer systems work. When I first looked at the tremendous amount of variety among the examples I had collected, it seemed as if there was no rhyme or reason to it. There was no way to understand, for example, why an electronic transfer system would work for Ford's Vehicle Operations plants but not for Bechtel's construction sites, or why BP encouraged people to travel in person to assist another team, while E&Y managed to provide very competent help to their teams by having colleagues just send in their "naturally occurring work products." It was not until I began to call upon my own tacit knowledge, born out of years of studying the theory and practice of learning in organizational settings, that I began to see the pattern in the examples. When I looked carefully at whether the knowledge involved in each example was tacit or explicit, whether the task involved was routine or nonroutine, and the extent to which the receiving teams had adequate absorptive capacity, I began to understand the *why* I had been searching for. The *why* led me to develop the five categories of transfer and to uncover the design principles that make each category work.

What I have done in building these categories is, of course, only a beginning. There is much more to know and much deeper to look at how organizational knowledge is created and how it can be effectively shared. I have offered several different examples of the ways organizations have implemented the guidelines within each transfer type, yet the near future will surely bring many additional and even more inventive ways to make each type of transfer work. Those new ways will help refine the guidelines and probably add to them as well.

We are very much at the front end of finding out how to make knowledge transfer work in organizations, and that seems both the promise and the constraint. The promise is that even these early attempts, based on little more than chance, have produced amazing results so that once we do gain a more systematic and complete understanding, the possibilities for increased productivity are phenomenal. The constraint is that we are a long way from that complete understanding yet.

In a sense this book is an attempt at Strategic Transfer of knowledge about transfer systems, if that is not too convoluted a notion. I am suggesting that organizations can learn from the experience of these successful organizations about how to construct systems that transfer common knowledge. But of course, they can't just do what the successful organizations did because making use of how others have implemented a knowledge transfer system is not a Near Transfer situation—it is Strategic Transfer.

I have tried in the book to follow my own guidelines for Strategic Transfer. To that end I have provided:

- a variety of cases and examples, each told in considerable detail and with attention to the context in which each system developed,

- a knowledge specialist (myself) from outside the organization to collect the data and construct the synthesis,

- a synthesis that retains the separate voices of the examples; the stories that begin each chapter are my attempt to preserve the emotions and values of the people involved by using their actual words,

- general principles derived from the cases that make up the five categories of transfer and the design guidelines for each, and

- an articulation of the reasoning behind the categories, which is the theory related to tacit and explicit knowledge, routine and nonroutine tasks, task similarity, and absorptive capacity, which formulate much of the *why* behind the categories.

But to complete the transfer receivers must now take these ideas and translate them into what is useful in their own situations, altering them in the process and surely improving upon them as well.

NOTES

CHAPTER 1
INTRODUCTION

1. David Constant, Sara Kiesler, and Lee Sproull, "What's Mine Is Ours, or Is It? A Study of Attitudes about Information Sharing," *Information Systems Research* 5, no. 4 (1994): 400–421.

2. Scott Cook and Dvora Yanow, "Culture and Organizational Learning," *Journal of Management Inquiry* 2, no. 4 (1993): 373–390.

CHAPTER 2
CREATING AND LEVERAGING COMMON KNOWLEDGE

1. Daniel A. Levinthal and James G. March, "The Myopia of Learning," *Strategic Management Journal* 14 (1993): 95–112.

2. John Seely Brown and Paul Duguid, "Organizational Learning and Communities of Practice: Toward a Unified View of Working, Learning, and Innovation," *Organization Science* 2 (1991): 40–57.

3. Wesley M. Cohen and Daniel A. Levinthal, "Absorptive Capacity: A New Perspective on Learning and Innovation," *Administrative Science Quarterly* 35 (1990): 128–152.

4. Gabriel Szulanski, "Unpacking Stickiness: An Empirical Investigation of the Barriers to Transfer Best Practice Inside the Firm," *Academy of Management Journal* 17 (1996): 437–441.

5. See Donald A. Schön, *The Reflective Practitioner* (New York: Basic Books, 1983); Chris Argyris, Robert Putnam, and Diana M. Smith, *Action Science* (San Francisco: Jossey-Bass, 1985); and Robert Kegan, *In Over Our Heads* (Cambridge, MA: Harvard University Press, 1994).

6. Michael Polanyi, *The Tacit Dimension* (Gloucester, MA: Peter Smith, 1983).

7. Geary A. Rummler and Alan P. Brache, *Improving Performance: How to Manage the White Space on the Organization Chart* (San Francisco: Jossey-Bass, 1990).

CHAPTER 3
SERIAL TRANSFER

1. Lloyd Baird, John C. Henderson, and Stephanie Watts, "Learning from Action: An Analysis of the Center for Army Lessons Learned (CALL)," *Human Resource Management* 36, no. 4 (1997): 385–395.

2. Nick Milton, "Knowledge with Shelf Life" (forthcoming). Milton uses the term "Serial Transfer" in this article, which describes BP's Knowledge Assets.

3. Nancy M. Dixon, "Hallways of Learning," *Organizational Dynamics* 25, no. 4 (Spring 1997): 23–34.

4. Daniel A. Levinthal and James G. March, "The Myopia of Learning," *Strategic Management Journal* 14 (1993): 95–112.

5. Christopher Meyer, "How the Right Measures Help Teams Excel," *Harvard Business Review* 72, no. 3 (May–June 1994): 95–103.

6. Chris Argyris, *Knowledge for Action: A Guide to Overcoming Barriers to Organizational Change* (San Francisco: Jossey-Bass: 1993).

CHAPTER 4
NEAR TRANSFER

1. Robert M. Gagne, *The Conditions of Learning and Theory of Instruction* (Austin, TX: Holt, Rinehart and Winston, 1997).

2. Gabriel Szulanski, "Unpacking Stickiness: An Empirical Investigation of the Barriers to Transfer Best Practice Inside the Firm," *Academy of Management Journal* 17 (1996): 437–441.

3. John Seely Brown and Paul Duguid, "Organizing Knowledge," *California Management Review* 40, no. 3 (Spring 1998): 90–111.

CHAPTER 5
FAR TRANSFER

1. S. K. Gupta, "Accelerating Excellence through Sharing Best Practices," Lockheed Martin White Paper (Washington, DC, 1999), p. 3.

2. Gupta, ibid.

3. Thomas H. Davenport and Laurence Prusak, *Working Knowledge* (Boston: Harvard Business School Press, 1998), p. 92.

4. Michael W. Macy, "Learning Theory and the Logic of Critical Mass," *American Sociological Review* 55 (1990): 809–826.

CHAPTER 6
STRATEGIC TRANSFER

1. Karl E. Weick, *Sensemaking in Organizations* (Thousand Oaks, CA: Sage, 1995).

2. Art Kleiner and George Roth, "How to Make Experience Your Company's Best Teacher," *Harvard Business Review* 75, no. 5 (September–October 1997): 172–177.

3. Kleiner and Roth, ibid.

4. George Roth and Art Kleiner, "Field Manual for the Learning Historian," The Learning History Research Project Web site, <http://ccs.mit.edu/lh/> (1998).

5. Nick Milton, "Knowledge with Shelf Life" (forthcoming).

6. Chris Argyris, *Knowledge for Action: A Guide to Overcoming Barriers to Organizational Change* (San Francisco: Jossey-Bass, 1993).

7. Stephanie A. Watts, James B. Thomas, and John C. Henderson, "Understanding 'Strategic Learning': Linking Organizational Learning, Sensemaking, and Knowledge Management" (paper presented at the Academy of Management Meeting, Boston, MA, 1997).

8. Weick, ibid., p. 28.

9. John Seely Brown and Paul Duguid, "Organizing Knowledge," *California Management Review* 40, no. 3 (Spring 1998): 90–111.

10. Roger C. Conant and Robert W. Ashby, "Every Good Regulator of a System Must Be a Model of That System," *International Journal of Systems Science* 1, no. 2 (1970): 89–97.

11. Kleiner and Roth, ibid., p. 3.

12. Milton, ibid.

CHAPTER 7
EXPERT TRANSFER

1. David Constant, Lee Sproull, and Sara Kiesler, "The Kindness of Strangers: The Usefulness of Electronic Weak Ties for Technical Advice, *Organization Science* 7, no. 2 (1996): 119–135.

2. Michael W. Macy, "Learning Theory and the Logic of Critical Mass," *American Sociological Review* 55 (1990): 809–826.

CHAPTER 8
LOOKING ACROSS THE FIVE TYPES OF KNOWLEDGE TRANSFER

1. Henry W. Chesbrough and David J. Teece, "When Is Virtual Virtuous? Organizing for Innovation," *Harvard Business Review* 74, no. 1 (January–February 1996): 65–73.

2. Jean Lave and Etienne Wenger, *Situated Learning: Legitimate Peripheral Participation* (New York: Cambridge University Press, 1991); Etienne Wenger, *Communities of Practice: Learning, Meaning, and Identity* (New York: Cambridge University Press, 1998).

3. Wenger, *Communities of Practice,* p. xiii.

4. David Bohm, *Unfolding Meaning: A Weekend of Dialogue with David Bohm* (New York: Ark Paperbacks, 1985).

5. Wenger, ibid., p. 10.

CHAPTER 9
BUILDING AN INTEGRATED SYSTEM FOR KNOWLEDGE TRANSFER

1. Robert H. Buckman, "Lions, Tigers, and Bears," Buckman Laboratories Knowledge Nurture Web site, <http://www.knowledge-nurture.com> (1997).

INDEX

AAR. *See* After Action Review
absorptive capacity, 24, 41, 65, 88,
    112, 134–135
action
    creation of common knowledge
        and, 18–19
    knowledge versus information and,
        13
    Near Transfer and, 67
After Action Review (AAR)
    at Bechtel, 39–42, 46
    at British Petroleum, 38–39, 45, 46,
        47
    group construction of knowledge
        and, 158
    in U.S. Army, 33–34, 37–38, 44,
        45, 47
Alert Notification System at TI,
    57–60, 66, 67, 69, 70, 71, 165
Argyris, Chris, 49
Ashby, Robert, 120–121

barriers to knowledge transfer

in Expert Transfer system, 139–140
in Far Transfer system, 93–95
in Near Transfer system, 72–74, 75
in Serial Transfer system, 46–50
in Strategic Transfer system,
    122–124
Bechtel, 14
    Clearinghouse, 2–3
    "lessons learned" meetings at, 29,
        39–42, 46
    name of knowledge-sharing system
        at, 9–10
    Steam Generator Replacement
        Group, 39–42, 46
best practice. *See* Best Practices Repli-
    cation at Ford; Chevron;
    Lockheed Martin, LM21 Best
    Practices at; Near Transfer
Best Practices Replication (BPR) at
    Ford, 4–6, 29, 53–54, 55–57,
    64–66, 67–68, 69, 70, 71
    distributed model and, 151–152
    elements of, 161–162, 164, 165
Bio-Tek Instruments, 43

ABOUT THE AUTHOR

Nancy M. Dixon is Associate Professor of Administrative Sciences at The George Washington University in Washington D.C. and serves as the Director for that program. She was formerly a member of the Human Resource Development graduate faculty at The University of Texas, Austin.

Dr. Dixon has made a substantial contribution to the understanding of organizational learning through her many books and articles. *The Organizational Learning Cycle: How We Can Learn Collectively,* Second Edition (Gower, 1999) focuses on learning at the system level. *Perspectives on Dialogue: Making Talk Developmental for Individuals and Organizations* (The Center For Creative Leadership, 1996) and *Dialogue at Work* (Lemos and Crane, 1998) continue that focus, as do over fifty articles that she has written.

She serves as an Editorial Reviewer for the *Human Resource Development Quarterly,* as a member of the Editorial Board for *Management Learning,* and as a member of the Editorial Advisory Board for the *Journal of Workplace Learning.*

Dr. Dixon has consulted to numerous companies in the United States and abroad including Unisys, Lockheed Martin,

General Electric Aircraft Engines, Canadian Centre for Management Development, the Federal Aviation Administration, Nippon Telegraph and Telephone Corporation (Japan), Ericsson, (Sweden), and Paradigm (Norway). She is a frequent speaker at conferences both in the United States and Europe.